Contents

D1299697

Preface

Grammar and Usage Simplified is a book on Standard English for the twenty-first century. This brief book is written not just for developmental students, but for all students who need to master the English language and become better writers. Filled with a great amount of essential information, it can be used as a resource book for English-speaking students. Its use will also benefit students who can speak and read some English, but who are unfamiliar with the English language.

Most students today need help when it comes to Standard English because many people who used to be considered role models for students have become rather careless using the English language. Although it is true that language is human-made and often changes, there are some consistencies, such as agreement of subject and verb and agreement of pronouns and their antecedents, that should be adhered to. My hope is that this book will help students become more confident in writing and speaking in Standard English.

Organization

Grammar and Usage Simplified is composed of 31 lessons that begin with fundamental material such as recognizing sentences and sentence fragments, as well as the kinds of punctuation that different types of sentences usually contain. The lessons in *Grammar and Usage Simplified* are based on graduated levels of difficulty, with each lesson building on the next. Every lesson presentation contains the lesson's objective, an explanation with examples, and at least two practice exercises with answers, so students can gain skill in learning the concepts being presented. Of course, teachers can use the practices in any way they deem fit. They may wish to use the practice exercises to determine if their students have mastered the presented concepts.

DOROTHY RUBIN

SPECIAL NOTE: Any instructor who would like extra audio supplemental material can send an e-mail to RubinD@TCNJ.edu.

LESSON 1
Recognizing Sentences

OBJECTIVE This lesson will help you recognize different types of sentences, as well as the difference between complete sentences and sentence fragments.

Read the following conversation.

"Have you heard the news?"

"No, what happened?"

"I've been accepted into college."

"That's great!"

"Please, don't tell Joshua. I want to surprise him."

"I won't."

When we speak and write, we use different kinds of sentences for different purposes.

- **Statement sentences** usually end in periods (.). "I've been accepted into college."
- **Question sentences** end in a (?). They often begin with such words as who, what, when, why, where, and how. "Who is she?"
- **Command sentences** are a direct order or make a polite request for someone to do something, and they generally end in a period. "Turn in your homework." "Please don't tell Joshua."
- The word **you** is understood in many sentences. "Go." "Stay."
- **Exclamatory sentences** express strong feeling and usually end with an exclamation point(!). "She is great!"

We write in complete sentences, but when we speak we may use sentence parts called **sentence fragments.**

"Have you talked to Erin?"

"Yes."

"What's she doing tonight?"

"Going to the dance."

"With you?"

"No, with Alfredo."

- A sentence must express a complete thought. **Examples:** The people are laughing. Studying is hard work. That is great!
- A sentence contains a word or group of words that names something about which something is said.
- A sentence may be as brief as one word. **Examples:** Go. Stay. Run. In the preceding sentences, the word *you* is understood.
- Sentence fragments are groups of words. **Examples:** Into the store. Running around. The study done. When they play.

Directions: Underline the complete sentences in the following list.

1. Stay here.
2. Go.
3. In the study.
4. Let's do it.
5. To get closer.
6. Jump.
7. The gasoline prices.
8. The terrorists are.
9. The World Trade Center, when the firefighters arrived.
10. That is the way life is.

Check answers on page 72.

PRACTICE B

Directions: For each of the following sentences, decide if the sentence is a statement, a question, a command, or an expression of great surprise or emotion. Then correctly punctuate each.

1. That is fantastic
2. Stay if you wish
3. Leave immediately
4. The terrorist attack against the World Trade Center will not be forgotten
5. My instructor is a pleasant individual
6. Help
7. Please stay with us
8. Who is that person
9. What does he want
10. How can we help

Check answers on page 72.

LESSON 2
Nouns

OBJECTIVE This lesson will help you recognize nouns.

Read the following sentences with missing words:

The —————— went to my ——————. The —————— scratched the ——————.

_____ works hard. A _____ bumped into _____.

My _____ is pretty. The _____, _____, and

_____ went into a _____.

Nouns are omitted from all the sentences to highlight the fact that without nouns, sentences would be difficult to read and write.

- **Nouns** are words that name persons, animals, places, things, or ideas. **Examples of nouns:** cat, animal, father, candy, sand, health, love, peace, kindness
- Nouns that name a particular person, place, or thing are called **proper nouns**. **Examples of proper nouns:** Marisa, Asia, United States, America, Ben
- Proper nouns always begin with a capital letter. **Examples:** Leslie, Africa, John
- Some nouns name a group, a class, or a collection that we consider as a whole or a unit. We call these **collective nouns. Examples:** class, group, clergy, party, flock, gang, crowd, family
- Nouns fit in a certain pattern or word order in a sentence; therefore, position is an important clue to help you determine if the word is a noun.
- Certain words signal that a noun follows. **Examples:** a, an, his, her, my, our, your, the. *a* brother, *an* apple, *his* mother, *her* dog, *my* brother, *our* house, *your* friend, *the* man.
- Certain endings may also signal a noun: **Examples:** *tion*—attention, *sion*—vision, *ance*—maintenance, *er*—writer, *or*—author, *ar*—beggar, *ness*—business, *ship*—governorship, *ment*—pavement, *ism*—imperialism, *ist*—vocalist, *ence*—reference, *ity*—clarity, *al*—rehearsal.

PRACTICE A

Directions: Fill in the following sentences with nouns.

1. My _____ is pretty.

2. Her _____ is mean.

3. _____ is a hard worker.

4. Our _____ is in trouble.

5. Is your _____ coming to the party?

6. Stop the _____.

7. The mean _____ scratched my _____.

8. The _____, _____, and _____ went into a _____.

9. A _____ bumped into the _____.

10. _____ likes to _____.

Check answers on page 72.

PRACTICE B

Directions: Write a noun for the following endings.

1. ism _____
2. ar _____
3. or _____
4. ence _____
5. ance _____

6. ship _____
7. al _____
8. tion _____
9. ity _____
10. sion _____

Check answers on page 72.

LESSON 3
Nouns in the Singular and Plural

OBJECTIVE This lesson will help you form the plural of nouns.

- In English, most nouns change their form for number. Nouns can be either singular or plural.
  - A **singular noun** refers to one person, place, animal, thing, or idea. **Examples:** Jose, Jennifer, bread, chair, toy, book
  - A **plural noun** refers to more than one person, place, animal, thing, or idea. **Examples:** three students, five dogs, two chairs, writers, ideas, loves
  - Most nouns add -**s** to make them plural. **Examples:** cats, hats, trees, trucks
  - Nouns that end in -*s, -ss, -sh, -ch,* or -*x* add -**es** to show the plural. **Examples:** buses or busses, dresses, benches, sashes, taxes, boxes, rashes, brushes
  - Nouns that end in -*y* preceded by a vowel, add -**s** to form the plural. **Examples:** boys, days, keys
  - Nouns that end in -*y* preceded by a consonant, change the *y* to **i** and add -**es** to form the plural. **Examples:** babies, candies, stories, worries
  - Nouns that end in -*f* or -*fe* are usually made plural by changing the *f* or *fe* to -**ves. Examples:** wives, knives, shelves
    - There are numerous exceptions to the *f* or *fe* noun generalization. Some nouns that end in -*f* or -*fe* add -**s** for their endings. **Examples:** chiefs, roofs, dwarfs, gulfs, safes
- Some nouns are the same in the singular and plural. **Examples:** salmon, deer, sheep
- Some nouns change their form in the plural. **Examples:** child—children, man—men, woman—women, tooth—teeth, mouse—mice, ox—oxen, goose—geese
- In addition, hyphenated compounds are made plural by making the most important word of the compound plural. **Examples:** brothers-in-law, attorneys-at-law, ladies-in-waiting, jacks-in-the-box
- If you are unsure of how the plural of a word is formed, it is a good idea to look it up in the dictionary.

PRACTICE A

Directions: Write the plural of the following words.

1. pass _____

2. clock _____

3. class _____

4. witch _____

5. dish _____

6. ax _____

7. pinch _____

8. fox _____

Check answers on page 72

PRACTICE B

Directions: Write the plural of the following words.

1. wife _____

2. father-in-law _____

3. deer _____

4. salmon _____

5. knife _____

6. roof _____

7. elf _____

8. sheep _____

9. lady-in-waiting _____

Check answers on page 72.

LESSON 4
Pronouns I

OBJECTIVE This lesson will help you recognize and begin to use pronouns correctly.

- It is very difficult to speak or write without using pronouns. Read the following paragraph, which avoids using pronouns: Frank told Dave that Frank would be late. Dave seemed upset about the situation. Why was Dave so upset? Emily didn't know, so Emily asked Dave.

  Now read the following sentences in the paragraph with pronouns: Frank told Dave that he would be late. Dave seemed upset about it. Why was he so upset? Emily didn't know, so she asked Dave.

- Needless to say, pronouns are a vital part of the English language.

- A **pronoun** is used in place of a noun. **Examples:** Mother and father are here. They are here. The pronoun **they** is used in place of mother and father.

- Pronouns are words such as *I, you, she, he, we, they, this, that, them, who, which, what, any, others, another, myself, himself, herself, each.*

PRACTICE A

Directions: State the pronoun(s) in the following sentences.

1. Melissa and her brother are in Jane's class. _____

2. What classes are you both taking? _____

3. Kelsey and I are taking biology. _____

4. Is she Jane's sister? _____

5. Does your instructor give lots of tests? _____

Check answers on page 72.

PRACTICE B

Directions: Write a pronoun that makes sense in the missing blank.

Kelsey was happy when (1) _____ was accepted to college. (2) _____ mother made a party to celebrate (3) _____ daughter's acceptance to college. At the party lots of people came and brought (4) _____ lots of things. Kelsey's boyfriend said that (5) _____ did not like the idea of Kelsey going away to college. (6) _____ felt that other guys would try to date (7) _____ because (8) _____ is very pretty and smart. Kelsey told (9) _____ not to worry. (10) _____ boyfriend, however, did.

Check answers on page 72.

LESSON 5
Pronouns II

OBJECTIVE This lesson should help you more in using pronouns correctly in sentences.

- In Lesson 4, you learned that pronouns are used in place of nouns.
- Pronouns like nouns, must agree with their verbs.
  - **Examples of singular pronouns:** I, you, he, she, it, me, him, her
  - **Examples of plural pronouns:** we, you, they, us, them
- There are a number of different types of pronouns, and pronouns may be used in different ways.
- The pronouns that you are probably the most familiar with and use the most often are those that indicate the person speaking, the person spoken to, or the person or thing spoken about.

- Examples of such pronouns:

I	we
you	you
he, she, it	they

  I refers to the first person and points out the person speaking. **You** refers to the second person or the person spoken to, and **he, she,** or **it** refers to the third person or thing spoken about. The same holds true for the plural.

- Some pronouns that are often used to point out the specific person or thing that is being referred to are **this, that, these,** and **those.** Examples: *That* is great. *Those* are great.

- Pronouns that are used in asking questions are **who, which,** and **what.** Examples: *What* is that? *Which* is that? *Who* are you? *What* are they doing? (**Note:** The pronoun *what* is treated similarly to the words *this is* and *these are;* see Lesson 14.)

- Some pronouns are used to refer to persons or things that are not easy to identify.

  Examples: anybody, somebody, nobody, anyone, anybody, no one, nobody.

  Examples in sentences: *Nobody* is here. *Somebody* is here. *Someone* has my book.

PRACTICE A

Directions: Insert a correct pronoun in the following sentences.

1. _____ am feeling ill today.

2. _____ is there?

3. _____ are the students doing?

4. Are _____ going to the party tomorrow?

5. _____ said that Hamid is handsome.

Check answers on page 72.

PRACTICE B

Directions: Put a C in the blank if the sentence is correct. If the sentence is not correct, write **NC** and write the sentence correctly. The first is done for you.

1. Somebody want to go. _NC   Somebody wants to go._____

2. Who is that? _____

3. What are those things? _____

4. He are happy. _____

5. We is not going to the party tomorrow. _____

6. The teacher said that someone was not doing the assignments. _____

7. I are happy. _____

8. We have too much work to do. _____

9. Who is there? _____

10. What do you want? _____

Check answers on page 72.

Pronouns III

OBJECTIVE This lesson should continue helping you to use pronouns correctly in sentences.

- When the pronoun **I** is used with another subject in a sentence, the *I* is presented last. **Example:** Erika and I are going to the party. (**Note:** The verb is plural because there is a compound subject in the sentence.)

- When a sentence has two pronouns, the verb in the sentence agrees with the pronoun that is used as the subject of the sentence. **Example:** She loves him. **Loves** agrees with the feminine singular subject **she**, the doer of the action. The masculine singular pronoun **him** is the object of the verb *loves;* in other words, *him* is receiving the action.

  - Forms of pronouns to use when the pronoun is the object of an action:

me	us
you	you
her, him, it	them

SPECIAL NOTE: The pronoun **you** remains the same in the singular and the plural.

- The same form of pronoun is used when the pronoun is the object of the action as when the pronoun follows a preposition, which are words such as *about, above, across, after, against, amid, among, around, at, beneath, between, down, for, from, up, upon, inside, over, off, on, to, with.* **Examples:** Give it *to* me. Is Stephanie *against* us? He accidentally went *into* me. It is *between* Mark and me. It is *beneath* him. Javaria is *with* me. The shelf *above* Kelsey fell on her.

  - When a preposition is followed by a noun or pronoun, the noun or pronoun is the receiver of the action, or the object of the preposition.

- It is also important to know that when the pronouns **who, what,** and **which** are used in asking questions, only the pronoun *who* changes its form based on how it is used in a sentence. When the pronoun **who** is the object of a preposition or used as the receiver of the action, it changes its form to **whom.** **Examples:** To *whom* are you speaking? With *whom* are you going? For *whom* are you working? About *whom* are you speaking?

Directions: In the following sentences, if the pronoun is correct, write **C** in the blank. If the pronoun is incorrect, write NC in the blank and insert the correct pronoun. The first is done for you.

1. To who are you speaking? <u>NC   whom</u>

2. The ball hit I. _____

3. The nurse gave she an injection. _____

4. John and me are going. _____

5. To who are you giving that? _____

6. Help us. _____

7. Listen to me. _____

8. Show I the dress. _____

9. Listen to whoever is in charge. _____

10. Please share that with us. _____

Check answers on page 72.

Directions: Insert the correct pronoun in the sentences below.

1. Give _____ the ball. (I or me)

2. To _____ did you say that? (who or whom)

3. Mary and _____ are going to the party. (I or me)

4. Between you and _____, let's not go.(I or me)

5. The block hit _____. (he or him)

Check answers on page 72.

LESSON 7
Pronouns IV

OBJECTIVE This lesson should continue to help you use pronouns correctly when you speak and write.

• In the previous lessons on pronouns, you learned that there are various types of pronouns and two of the major ways in which pronouns are used in a sentence. This lesson will show you another important way to use pronouns.

• Pronouns are used to show **possession**, that is, ownership or belonging. Read the following sentences:

I am going to my car.	Do not open my mail.
Her coat is here.	Here is our subscription.
His coat is there.	The dog is wagging its tail.
My name is Craig.	Is that book yours?
Put my mail on the table.	No, your book is here.

In the sentence *I am going to my car,* **my** is the pronoun showing ownership. The pronoun *my* shows that the car belongs to me.

In the sentence *Her coat is here,* the pronoun **her** shows that the coat belongs to a female.

Now read the sentence *Is that book yours?* The pronoun **yours** asks whether the book belongs to you.

You should recognize by now that pronouns showing ownership are important for communication.

Here are the forms of pronouns that are used to show possession or ownership:

my, mine	our, ours
your, yours	your, yours
her, his	their, theirs

Here are sentences using some pronouns:

1. I need my textbook. (The pronoun *my* shows to whom the textbook belongs.)
   That textbook is mine. (The pronoun *mine* shows the textbook belongs to me.)
2. Take your book. (The pronoun *your* shows to whom the book belongs.)
   This book is yours. (The pronoun *yours* shows that the book belongs to you.)

You can also show ownership by saying or writing it in the following way: The textbook belongs to me. This sentence is the same as saying the textbook is mine.

Here are some more examples:

1. The book belongs to you.
   The book is yours.
2. The book belongs to her.
   The book is hers.

In the previous lesson, you learned that of the pronouns *who, which,* and *what,* only *who* changes its form when it is the object of a preposition or of an action. When the pronoun **who** is used to show a question of ownership or a question of belonging, **who** changes its form to **whose. Examples:** *Whose* house is that? *Whose* book is that?

PRACTICE A

Directions: Insert the correct pronoun in the blank.

1. To _____ does that belong? (who, whom)

2. _____ both do not want to go to Mark's party. (I, we, us)

3. _____ boat is that? (Who, Whose)

4. Is that _____? (your, yours)

5. Between _____ and me, I really don't want to go. (she, her)

Check answers on page 72.

PRACTICE B

Directions: If the sentence is correct, write **C** in the blank; if it is not correct, write **NC** in the blank and insert the correct pronoun.

1. To whom does that textbook belong? _____

2. Who are you going to see? _____

3. Is that yours? _____

4. Between you and I, she is not very nice. _____

5. Is that for her? _____

Check answers on page 72.

Summary of Pronouns and Their Uses
Lessons 4–7

A pronoun is used in place of a noun. **Examples:** Melissa is pretty. She is pretty.

- There are different types of pronouns. **Examples:** I, you, this, that, who, anyone
- Some pronouns change their form to show person. **Examples:** I, you, he, she, it, we, they.
- Some pronouns change their form based on how they are used in a sentence.
  - Subject of a sentence—I, you, she, he, it, we, you, they.
  - As receiver of the action or object of the verb—me, you, her, him, it, us, you, them, as well as after prepositions—to, with, against, between, before.
  - To show ownership or belonging—my, mine; you, his, hers, its; our, ours; your, yours; their, theirs
- When used in question sentences, the pronoun **who**, changes its form:
  - As subject—**who**
  - As receiver of action or after a preposition—**whom**
  - As a word that shows ownership—**whose**

LESSON 8
Pronouns and Agreement, Including Sexism

OBJECTIVE This lesson will show that pronouns must agree with their antecedent, that is, the nouns or pronouns they refer to.

Pronouns are frequently used incorrectly in speaking and writing.

Some Rules to Follow Concerning Pronouns and Agreement

- When a pronoun replaces or refers to a singular noun, the pronoun must be singular. **Examples:** The swing is too high. *It* is too high. Maria is pretty. *She* is pretty.

- Words such as *each, anybody, every, everybody, either, neither, everyone, no one, somebody, man,* and *woman* require a singular pronoun. **Examples:** Everyone must do what he or she thinks is right. (The singular pronouns *he* and *she* refer to the pronoun *everyone.*)

SPECIAL NOTE: To avoid sexism, use the pronouns **he** or **she** or **his** or **her.** Years ago, only the masculine pronoun **he** was used rather than the feminine and masculine pronouns. **Examples:** *Everyone* must do what *he* thinks is correct. Presently, some writers and speakers use the plural **their** as antecedents for singular pronouns. They write: *Everyone* must do what *they* think is correct. Since language changes, eventually this may become correct usage; however, currently it is still not good usage to use a plural pronoun to refer to a singular noun or pronoun.

- When a pronoun replaces or refers to a plural noun, the pronoun must be plural. **Examples:** My cat and dog eat *their* food slowly. My dogs scratch *their* backs a lot.

PRACTICE A

Directions: Underline the correct pronoun for the following sentences.

1. Although the apartment is lovely, (it/their) is too small for my family.

2. Neither Joshua nor Taylor has received (his/their) grades yet.

3. My uncle and my father finished (his/their) work.

4. Everybody is working on (his or her/their) English theme.

5. The children asked (his or her/their) mother if (he or she/they) could go to the movies.

6. Neither Mary nor Megan has eaten (her/their) dinner yet.

7. Each person must decide for (himself or herself/themselves or theirselves) what to do with (his or her/their) life.

8. The two girls told (his/their) teacher that (she/they) would help (her/them.)

9. Nobody is able to predict what (his or her/their) life has in store for (him or her/them.)

10. The crowd as one cheered on (its/their) favorite team.

Check answers on page 72.

PRACTICE B

Directions: Fill in each blank with the correct pronoun.

1. All my friends obtained _____ drivers' licenses.

2. Not one person I know has _____ own car.

3. Neither of our friends owned _____ own car.

4. Some wild animals will breed only in _____ natural environment.

5. The hunters lost _____ way.

6. Jennifer asked _____ mother if _____ could spend the night in _____ friend's house.

7. Not everyone takes good care of _____ room.

8. Not one person in _____ driver education course class failed _____ driving test.

9. _____ dorm rooms are really not too nice.

10. The students said that _____ needed more time to finish _____ units.

Check answers on page 72.

REVIEW PRACTICE ON PRONOUNS

Directions: In the blank at the end of each sentence, put a **C** if the sentence is correct. If the sentence is not correct, write **NC** in the blank and rewrite the sentence correctly.

Example: Not one of us are going to change our mind. _NC   Not one of us is going to change_
              his or her mind.

1. Everybody knew beforehand what they was supposed to say. _____

2. Although Mary worked her way through school, she was not prepared for the difficulties that awaited her. _____

3. If you see anyone I know, please tell them "hello" for me. _____

4. Neither John nor Carlos are going to the party. _____

5. Each of the studies is evaluated on its own merits. _____

Check answers on page 72.

OBJECTIVE This lesson will help you use subjects of sentences correctly.

You learned in the lesson on nouns that nouns change their meaning based on their position in a sentence. **Examples:** The man bit the dog. The dog bit the man. In the first and second sentences both *man* and *dog* are nouns, but in the first sentence only the noun *man* is the subject of the sentence. **Man** is the doer of the action. The **dog** is receiving the action. **Dog** is the object of what the **man** is doing. In the second sentence, the **dog** is the subject of the sentence, and the **man** is receiving the action.

- The **subject of a sentence** is a word or group of words about which something is said.
- A subject can be either a noun or a pronoun.
- A sentence can have a single (one subject only) or plural (more than one) subject:

  Examples (single subjects): he, it, mother, brother, father, son

  Examples (plural subjects): they, them, men, women, children, employers, hopes
- Two or more subjects joined by the word **and** are called **compound subjects** and are usually plural. **Examples:** Bread, butter, *and* jam taste good. Ben *and* I are friends.
- The subject of a sentence can be a person, an animal, place, thing, or idea.
- The subject usually appears at the beginning of a sentence before the verb and before the other nouns in the sentence.
- A sentence consists of a subject and verb.
- When you speak and write in English, there must be agreement between the subject and verb in a sentence. More will be written about this very important point beginning in Lesson 12.

PRACTICE A

Directions: State the single, compound, or plural subject in the following sentences.

1. Speedy lost his license because of speeding. _____

2. Now, Jim and I drive Speedy to school every day. _____

3. It is really a pain in the neck to have to pick Speedy up. _____

4. He does not appreciate what we have given up _____

5. We used to jog every day. _____

6. Each of us believes that exercise is good for you. _____

7. A good breakfast is also important. _____

8. Now we hardly have time for breakfast. _____

9. Speedy thinks that we are being poor sports. _____

10. Speedy and his friends keep saying that we are not behaving "cool." _____

Check answers on page 72.

PRACTICE B

Directions: Determine if the subject in the sentences in Practice A is a singular or plural subject. Write **S** for singular and **P** for plural.

1. _____   6. _____

2. _____   7. _____

3. _____   8. _____

4. _____   9. _____

5. _____   10. _____

Check answers on page 72.

LESSON 10
Verbs

OBJECTIVE This lesson should help you recognize the importance of verbs in a sentence.

Read the following sentences with missing words. Do they make sense?

I _____ school. What _____ to you last night? Where

_____ you _____?

Peter _____ hard and _____ hard. _____ he in

you class?

The presented sentences are all missing verbs. The verb is usually a key word in the sentence because it clears up meaning. It also often adds sparkle to your sentence if you use a descriptive verb. **Example:** *The horse galloped out of the stable* sounds better than *The horse rode out of the stable* or *The horse came out of the stable.*

- **Verbs** are telling words; they tell about anything that happens or takes place.
- Verbs express action, a state of being.
- Verbs can be one word. **Examples:** Javaria *works* all the time. Melissa and Kelsey *are* sisters. *Go* there. The West Nile mosquito *bit* me.
- Some sentences have two or more verbs (**compound verbs**). **Example:** Peter *works* and *plays* hard.

- Predicates refer to verbs; a **predicate** may be a single word or a group of words. **Examples:** She *works*. She *has been working*.
  - A **simple predicate** contains only the verb or the verb phrase (see Lesson 11).
  - The **complete predicate** contains the verb or verb phrase with everything that follows the verb or verb phrase. **Example:** She *has been working very hard for a long time*. The words in italics are the complete predicate.
- Verbs, like nouns, have some special endings to signal that the word is a verb. **Examples:** *-ize, -ify, -en*. The noun *economy* becomes the verb *economize;* the word *beautiful* becomes the verb *beautify;* the word *hard* becomes the verb *harden.*
- Verbs agree with their subject(s).
  - Forms of verbs tell us whether they are singular or plural. **Examples:** Pat *eats* too much. Mohammid and Hamil *eat* too much. The forms for regular verbs with pronouns follow:

I play	we play
you play	you play
he, she, or it plays	they play

  - Generalizations to remember in Standard English:
    - With singular subjects that are nouns, you usually add *-s* or *-es* to the verb. **Examples:** The cat meow*s*. The dog bark*s*.
    - With plural subjects that are nouns, you usually add nothing to the verb. **Examples:** The cats meow. The dogs bark.

> **CAUTION:** Do not confuse the singular and plural form of nouns with those of verbs. Remember that most nouns add an **-s** or **-es** to form the plural. **Examples:** one *cat*, two *cats*; one *bush*, two *bushes*.
>
> Verbs, however, usually add an **-s** or **-es** to form the singular. **Examples:** The cat *runs*. Two persons *run*.

  - With the singular pronouns **I** and **you**, we use the verb form that is used with plural subjects. **Examples:** I walk; you walk. I talk; you talk. I eat; you eat.

PRACTICE A

Directions: For each of the following nouns and pronouns, write the correct form of the verb.

1. dogs barks _____
2. students runs _____
3. she play _____
4. they plays _____
5. we plays _____
6. I plays _____
7. it run _____
8. You naps _____
9. Helps me _____
10. Saves her _____

Check answers on page 72.

Directions: Write the verbs *run, play,* and *work* for the singular pronouns *I* and *you.*

1. I _____

2. I _____

3. I _____

4. you _____

5. you _____

6. you _____

Check answers on page 72.

LESSON 11
Verbs as Groups of Words

OBJECTIVE This lesson will help you recognize groups of words and how to use the verbs **to be** and **to have.**

- Read the following: My instructor *has helped* me a lot. In the sentence *has helped* is considered a group of words. Often verbs have **helping verbs** to express better what is taking place. At this point it is important to state that the English language can be confusing. However, if you learn some basic generalizations, you should do well.

- Predicates refer to verbs. A **predicate** may be a single word or a group of words. **Examples:** She *works.* She *has been working.*

- We call groups of words **verb phrases.** The following groups of words in italics are verb phrases. I *am going.* She *has seen* them. Marisa *will be going.* Peter *may go* with us. They *did know* her. (In the verb phrases, *am, has seen, will be, may,* and *did* are helping verbs.)

  - When helping verbs accompany a verb, they give the time, number, and so forth of the verb. **Examples:** She *will arrive* tomorrow. *Have* you *seen* Marisa?

- A simple predicate contains only the verb or the verb phrase.

- The complete predicate contains the verb or verb phrase with everything that follows the verb or verb phrase. **Example:** She *has been working very hard for a long time.* The words in italics are the complete predicate.

- The helping words *to be* and *to have* are used very often with other verbs. **Examples:** She *has work* to do. I *am going* to the party tonight.

- The verbs *to be* and *to have* can be used alone as the complete verb. **Examples:** The box *is* full. I *have* enough work. Who *is* she? I *have* the pizza. He *has* lots of money.

- Here are the forms of the verb *to be* used with singular and plural subjects.

  The box *is*

  The boxes *are*

  The student *is*

  The students *are*

- Here are the forms of the verb *to be* used with pronouns when *to be* is used alone as the complete verb:

  I *am* here.   We *are* here.

  You *are* here.   You *are* here.

  He, she, or it *is* here.   They *are* here.

- Here are the forms of the verb *to be* used with pronouns when *to be* is used as a helping verb.

  I *am jogging*.   We *are jogging*.

  You *are jogging*.   You *are jogging*.

  He, she, or it *is jogging*.   They *are jogging*.

- Here are the forms of the verb *to have* used with pronouns when *have* is used alone as the complete verb.

  I *have* it.   We *have* it.

  You *have* it.   You *have* it.

  She, he, or it *has* it.   They *have* it.

- Here are the forms of the verb *to have* used with pronouns when *have* is used as a helping verb.

  I *have jogged* today.   We *have jogged* today.

  You *have jogged* today.   You *have jogged* today.

  She, he, or it *has jogged* today.   They *have jogged* today.

PRACTICE A

Directions: Underline the verb phrases in each of the following sentences.

1. Pedro and his sister are going to a party.

2. Melissa is having a sleepover at her house.

3. He has been jogging for an hour.

4. I had jogged yesterday.

5. The men in our class are studying hard.

Check answers on page 72.

PRACTICE B

Directions: Here are verbs and subjects. Write the correct form for each.

Example: run; man _____Man runs_____

1. cry; baby _____

2. go; they _____

3. do; he _____

4. have; she _____

5. say; we _____

6. be; she _____

7. wish; I _____

8. wish; they _____

9. have; she _____

10. be; he _____

Check answers on page 72.

Agreement of Subject and Verb I

OBJECTIVE Almost all the lessons up to now should have prepared you for this lesson and the following ones on agreement of subject and verb.

- A subject and its verb should **agree in number.**
- When the subject in a sentence is a single noun or pronoun, naming only one thing or person, the subject is **singular. Examples:** student, idea, person, he or she, it.
- When the subject in a sentence names more than one thing or person, the subject is **plural. Examples:** students, ideas, people, they.
- Compound subjects are plural. **Examples:** Fred and Jack; Marisa, Molly, and Javaria.
- A singular subject requires a **singular verb.** Remember, singular verbs end in **s** or **es. Examples:** Seth jogs. Hammil sings. Sara rushes.
- A plural subject requires a **plural verb. Examples:** Fred and Jack jog. Milk, cheese, and yogurt are good sources of calcium.

PRACTICE A

Directions: In the following sentences, put **C** for correct in the blank if the sentence has the proper agreement between the subject and verb. Put **NC** if the agreement is incorrect and then put in the correct verb.

Example: My friends is going to the rock concert tonight. __NC___ *is going* should be *are going*__

1. My boss want me to work late today. _____

2. My brother and father are going fishing. _____

3. My sister has too many boyfriends. _____

4. Kelly and Shannon is buying a car. _____

5. Seth and Dan seems to know what to do. _____

6. I be going. _____

7. Leslie and Peter are buying a car. _____

8. David know what to do. _____

9. Who are you? _____

10. We is going soon. _____

Check answers on page 72.

Directions: Insert the correct verb in the following sentences.

1. It _____ hard working and trying to raise a family. (is , are)

2. Melissa and her sister _____ their mother a lot. (helps, help)

3. Andrew _____ a good swimmer and scuba diver. (is, are)

4. Many women _____ outside the home today. (works, work)

5. Numerous men _____ around the house today. (helps, help)

Check answers on page 72.

LESSON 13
Agreement of Subject and Verb II

OBJECTIVE This lesson deals with certain pronouns that require a singular verb.

- Pronouns such as *everybody, everyone, anyone, someone, no one, not one, somebody, anybody, nobody, everybody, neither,* and *either* are pronouns that take a singular verb. **Examples:** Everybody *is* present. No one *has* a ticket. Neither *is* welcome. Nobody *does* it correctly. Someone *has* my coat. No one *drives* my car but me.

PRACTICE A

Directions: For the following sentences, put a **C** for correct in the blank if the sentence has the proper agreement between the pronoun subject and verb. Put **NC** if the agreement is not correct and then put in the correct verb.

Example: Everyone were invited to my party. <u>NC   the verb *were* should be *was.*</u>

1. Someone are going. _____

2. Everybody is welcome. _____

3. Nobody know him. _____

4. Everybody work hard at the plant. _____

5. Somebody is supposed to do the work. _____

Check answers on page 72.

PRACTICE B

Directions: Insert the correct form of the verb for the following pronouns.

1. Someone _____ (is, are)

2. No one _____ (do, does)

3. Everybody _____ (has, have)

4. Somebody _____ (cooks, cook)

5. Neither _____ (know, knows)

Check answers on page 72.

LESSON 14
Agreement of Subject and Verb III

OBJECTIVE This lesson continues with more information on agreement of subject and verbs and should help you use the correct form of the verb with such subjects.

- The words **there is** should be followed by a singular noun. **Example:** *There is my friend*, Kelsey.

- The words **there are** should be followed by a plural noun. **Example:** *There are my friends*, Kelsey and Drew.

- Certain special subjects such as the *name of a television show, a book, a poem, a newspaper, a film*, and *a play* require a singular verb. **Examples:** The movie *Gone with the Wind* is a classic. *War and Peace* is a famous novel about Russia. The poem *Fog* by Carl Sandburg is very short. Shakespeare's *King Lear* is a famous play.

- There are some nouns such as *mathematics, physics, civics, ethics, measles, mumps* that are plural in form but require a singular verb. **Examples:** *Physics deals* with light, sound, heat, electricity, and matter in motion. *Mumps is* usually a childhood disease. *Mathematics is* a language. *Measles is* usually a dangerous disease for pregnant women. (Refer to a current dictionary when in doubt.)

- Certain special nouns such as *eyeglasses* or *spectacles, scissors, pants, athletics*, and *riches* are plural in form and require a plural verb. **Examples:** My *pants are* dirty. My *scissors have* sharp points.

- Some collective nouns such as *class, clergy, party, flock, gang, jury, crowd, company, family*, and *choir* that name a class, a group, or a collection are considered as a unit or a whole when acting as a unit.

  - When such nouns are in a sentence, we may use either a singular or plural verb with the noun depending on the meaning we wish to convey.

    - If we are thinking of the word *class* as a whole, we would use a singular verb. **Example:** The *class is* sending Melissa a get-well card.

    - If we are thinking of the word *class* as one made up of many separate individuals, we would use a plural verb. **Example:** The *class are* sending many thank-you notes.

Directions: Insert the correct verb or phrase in the following sentences.

1. _____ my sister. (There is/There are)

2. _____ my sisters. (There is/There are)

3. _____ Kelsey and Melissa. (There is/There are)

4. Civics _____ the study of the workings of the national government. (is/are)

5. Measles _____ very contagious for me. (is/are)

6. Riches _____ easy to obtain. (is/are)

7. My scissors _____ for a left-handed person. (is/are)

8. The play *Hamlet* _____ a classic. (is/are)

9. The book *War and Peace* _____ also a classic. (is/are)

10. *USA Today* _____ a national newspaper. (is/are)

Check answers on page 72.

Directions: Insert the correct verb or phrase in the following sentences.

1. Many students _____ economics in college. (take/takes)

2. Each year my class _____ a party to help the needy. (gives/give)

3. My company _____ sending me on a business trip. (is/are)

4. Our choir _____ singing to help worthy causes. (is/are)

5. Please _____ my pants. (press/presses)

6. My scissors _____ me. (cut/cuts)

7. My spectacles _____ dirty. (is/are)

8. Every year the choir _____ invitations to family members. (send/sends)

9. Ethics _____ with morals. (deal/deals)

10. Mathematics _____ a language. (is/are)

Check answers on page 72.

LESSON 15
Agreement of Subject and Verb IV

OBJECTIVE This lesson continues with even more information on agreement of subjects and verbs and should help you use the correct form of the verb with special subjects.

- When the word **each** is used with singular nouns connected by *and,* the verb is singular. **Example:** *Each boy and each girl is* able to play this game.
- When two or more singular subjects are connected by **or** or **nor**, the verb is usually singular. **Examples:** Neither Yolanda *nor* Peter *is* going. Either your dorm room *or* my dorm room *is* a good place for the party. Neither my brother, *nor* my sister, *nor* my cousin *is* invited to my party.
- When two subjects in a sentence are joined by **or** or **nor** and one subject is singular, and another subject is plural, the verb agrees with the subject closest to it. **Examples:** Neither my brother *nor sisters are going* to the party. Neither my sisters *or brother is going* to the party. Neither my dresses *nor sweater has been cleaned.* Neither my sweater *nor dresses have been cleaned.*
- The word **it** requires a singular verb. **Examples:** *It is* snowing today. *It is* nice outside.

PRACTICE A

Directions: Insert the correct verb in the following sentences.

1. It _____ not ready yet. (is/are)

2. Each man and each woman _____ present. (is/are)

3. Neither my cat nor dog _____ been fed. (has/have)

4. Either my brother or sisters _____ going to the hotel. (is/are)

5. Each of my friends _____ going to class. (is/are)

6. Either Hamid or Katie _____ having the party. (is/are)

7. Neither the sororities nor fraternities _____ going to your party. (is/are)

8. Neither my brother nor my cousin _____ going to your party. (is/are)

9. It _____ good. (sound/sounds)

10. Each pen and each pencil _____ damaged. (is/are)

Check answers on page 72.

PRACTICE B

Directions: Put a **C** in the blank if the sentence is correct. If the sentence is incorrect, write the correct verb. The first two are done for you.

1. Neither my house nor my sister's house *are* a ranch. __Is_____

2. The employees, together with their employer, are settling their differences. __C_____

3. It are not ready. _____

4. It has stopped snowing. _____

5. Neither his luggage nor my luggage is here. _____

6. Neither my relatives nor my foes are being invited._____

7. My shoes and socks are here. _____

8. Either Melissa or Kelsey is going. _____

9. That lesson and this one are good ones. _____

10. Each student and each tutor is present. _____

Check answers on page 72.

Check answers on page 72.

LESSON 16
Agreement of Subject and Verb V

OBJECTIVE This is the last lesson in this series on agreement of subjects and verbs. It should also help you use the correct form of the verb with special subjects.

- The word **all** may be either singular or plural based on the meaning we wish to convey. If we wish *all* to refer to the whole amount of something, the verb is singular. If, however, we wish *all* to refer to various individuals or things, the verb is plural. **Examples:** All of us are here. (*All* is plural because it refers to each and every person.) All is forgiven. All is forgotten. (*All* is singular because it means the whole amount.)

- The word **none** may also have a singular or plural verb based on the meaning that the writer or speaker wishes to express. However, the plural form of the verb is used most often with *none*. If writers of speakers wish to convey the singular, they generally use **no one, not one,** or **nobody. Examples:** None *are* here. Not one person *is* here. No one *is* here. Nobody *is* here.

- When a sentence has both a positive and negative subject, the verb agrees with the positive subject. **Examples:** You, not she, are going. He, not I, is going. I, not they, am going. We, not she, have the best seats. They, not he, are going to the party.

- When a sentence has a singular or plural subject with words that describe the subject, the verb is not influenced by the words that describe the subject. **Examples:** The researcher of these studies is well-known. The strength of the materials is important. These kinds of medicine are not dangerous. The children of Mrs. Johnson play here.

- When a subject is joined to other words by words such as *with, together, including, or, as well as,* the verb agrees with the subject and is not influenced by the words joined to the subject. **Examples:** My *sister, as well as* my brother, *is going.* My *friends, as well as* my sister, *are going.* My *brother and sister, together with* my friend Dave, *are going.* The *babysitter, together with* the children, *is* also *going* to the party.

PRACTICE A

Directions: Insert the correct verb in the following sentences.

1. All _____ not lost. (is/are)

2. Not one of us _____ available. (is/are)

3. Not one of her friends _____ fair. (play/plays)

4. Not one of them _____ available. (is/are)

5. All of my friends _____ home frequently. (write/writes)

6. She, not they, _____ going. (is/are)

7. Nobody _____ arrived yet. (has/have)

8. Bread, with jam and butter, _____ what I eat a lot of. (is/are)

9. I, not my best friend, _____ going away. (am/are)

10. The tenants of the building _____ to strike. (refuse/refuses)

Check answers on page 72.

PRACTICE B

Directions: Put a **C** in the blank if the sentence is correct. If the sentence is incorrect, write the correct verb. The first is done for you.

1. The employees, together with their employer, are settling their differences. _C_____

2. Not one of them have arrived. _____

3. The value of the studies are great. _____

4. The employees of this company has many benefits. _____

5. What kind of person are you? _____

6. All is right with the world. _____

7. My roommates, together with their significant others, are going on vacation. _____

8. The goat, as well as the cows, on my farm give milk. _____

9. That girl, not the adults, have the answer. _____

10. Five men claims she is telling the truth. _____

Check answers on page 72.

Review Practices
Lessons 1–16

If you get one or more items incorrect when there are only five items in the practice, I suggest strongly that you go back and review the material in that particular lesson.

LESSON 1: RECOGNIZING SENTENCES, SENTENCE FRAGMENTS, AND TYPES OF SENTENCES

A. Directions: Write **S** *or* **SF** in the blank. S = complete sentence; SF = sentence fragment.

1. Come here. _____
2. Go. _____
3. Who are you? _____
4. Running around. _____
5. Because of them. _____

6. Out of the dorm. _____
7. And she. _____
8. This is good. _____
9. Help. _____
10. What is that? _____

B. Directions: Punctuate the following sentences correctly.

1. What a nerve my roommate has
2. Please take me with you
3. Stop that now
4. Do I have an alternative
5. Have you considered the consequences of your actions

LESSON 2: NOUNS

Directions: Underline all the nouns in the following sentences. (Include proper nouns.)

1. Maria played the tune again.
2. John passed the butter.
3. The poor fox in the hunt looked for a place to hide.
4. The boys played a horrible trick on Maria.
5. Hannah hates tomatoes.
6. Seth loves to eat cheese.
7. Anna is my roommate at college.
8. Did Jim buy Erin roses?
9. The flowers are not looking too well.
10. Is Sharon's cell phone broken?

LESSON 3: NOUNS IN THE SINGULAR AND PLURAL

Directions: Make each of the following words plural.

1. Jones _____

2. bunch _____

3. Smith _____

4. Johnson _____

5. rash _____

6. tray _____

7. volley _____

8. leaf _____

9. monarchy _____

10. mother-in-law _____

LESSONS 4–8: PRONOUNS

A. Directions: Underline the pronouns in the following sentences.

1. My brother and I are going away to college in the fall.

2. My sister, Megan, is not too happy about where she is going.

3. Megan and John are twins who do things together, but they are going to different colleges.

4. It will be lonely with the two of them away.

5. It is good that we have such a large family.

B. Directions: Insert a correct pronoun in the following sentences.

1. _____ is not happy.

2. _____ are not going.

3. Please, give that to _____.

4. Hamill and _____ are going to the party.

5. Nora said that _____ cannot go with _____.

C. Directions: In the blank at the end of each sentence, put a **C** if the sentence is correct. If the sentence is not correct, write **NC** in the blank and rewrite the sentence correctly.

Example: Not one of us are going to change our mind. _NC_ Not one of us is going to change
his or her mind.

1. Everybody knew beforehand what they was supposed to say. _____

_____

2. Mary worked her way through school, but she was not prepared for the difficulties that

awaited her. _____

_____

3. If you see anyone I know, please tell him or her "hello" for me. _____

_____

4. Neither John nor Carlos are going to the party. _____

_____

5. Each of the studies is evaluated on its own merits. _____

_____

LESSON 9: SUBJECT OF A SENTENCE

Directions: Underline the word that is the subject in the following sentences. Then state in the blank whether the subject is a singular or plural.

1. Several huge dogs attacked my friend. _____

2. At first, nobody was available to help him. _____

3. My friend was badly hurt. _____

4. Some passersby finally walked by and helped me. _____

5. They called 911 for help. _____

LESSON 10: VERBS

Directions: Underline the verb(s) in the following sentences.

1. The basketball star at our school broke his arm.

2. My friends and I are practicing our skits for the school show.

3. They have gone with everyone to the picnic.

4. Jose and Jim played in the basketball game but lost.

5. Do you have to work hard in that course?

LESSON 11: VERBS AS GROUPS OF WORDS

Directions: Here are subjects and verbs. Put them together correctly.

1. be; you _____

2. have; it _____

3. you; be _____

4. be; I _____

5. be; it _____

LESSON 12: AGREEMENT OF SUBJECT AND VERB I

Directions: Underline the correct verb in the following sentences.

1. Jack, Pedro, Jamaal, and I (are/is) good friends.

2. We (read/reads) two books a week for our English literature course.

3. The branches and leaves (is/are) all over our walkway.

4. Erika and I (go/goes) to the same school.

5. I (am/are) happy here.

LESSON 13: AGREEMENT OF SUBJECT AND VERB II

Directions: Underline the correct verb.

1. Everyone (get/gets) the same treatment here.

2. No one (has/have) a ticket.

3. Everybody (want/wants) to go.

4. Nobody (is/are) at school today.

5. Neither (is/are) happy about that.

LESSON 14: AGREEMENT OF SUBJECT AND VERB III

Directions: Underline the correct verb.

1. There (is/are) too many people at the party.

2. There (is/are) my friends.

3. *Leave It To Beaver* and other old-time shows (is/are) making a comeback.

4. *King Lear* (is/are) a famous Shakespearean play.

5. *Mr. Murder* (is/are) a novel by Dean Koontz.

LESSON 15: AGREEMENT OF SUBJECT AND VERB IV

Directions: Underline the correct verb.

1. Either you or I will (play/plays.)

2. Each student (is/are) happy.

3. Each child and each mother (is/are) going on the picnic.

4. It (is/are) raining today.

5. Neither my best friend nor my siblings (like/likes) my decision.

LESSON 16: AGREEMENT OF SUBJECT AND VERB V

Directions: Underline the correct verb.

1. Not one of the children (is/are) here.

2. My friend, together with his siblings, (is/are) going to our party.

3. All (is/are) present.

4. Everyone is/are going to the party.

5. My brother, as well as his colleagues, (was/were) recently here.

Check answers for review assessment on pages 72–73.

LESSON 17

Simple and Compound Sentences, Including Information on Coordinate Conjunctions and Run-on Sentences

OBJECTIVE This lesson will help you recognize and write simple and compound sentences.

In Lesson 1, you learned about sentences and sentence fragments. This lesson expands on Lesson 1.

- A **simple sentence** contains a word or group of words that names something (subject) and says something about the thing named (verb). It expresses a complete thought. **Examples:** The World Trade Center was attacked by terrorists. I am a freshman.

- A simple sentence consists of one single statement, command, wish, question, or exclamation. **Examples:** Lydia is an excellent student. That is great! Who is he? Stay here.

- A simple sentence may be as brief as one word if it expresses a complete thought. **Examples:** Go. Stay. Help! Scream.

- A simple sentence may have a single subject and single verb or a compound (two or more) subject and compound verb. **Examples:** *Andrew is going* to Australia. The *faculty and students are going* to Belgium. The *students are going* to New York City and Maine. *Andrew and Mike are going* to Paris and London in the summer.

- A **compound sentence** is made up of two or more simple sentences. **Examples:** The World Trade Center doesn't exist anymore. It was attacked by terrorists on September 11, 2001. The World Trade Center doesn't exist anymore, for it was attacked by terrorists on September 11, 2001.

- Two simple sentences may be joined by certain linking words called **conjunctions** to form a *compound sentence*. Conjunctions that connect groups of words that have the same importance are called **coordinate conjunctions.** The most often used coordinate conjunctions are *and, but, or, nor, for,* and *yet.* The linking word *and* is used to connect one idea to another. *But* and *yet* are used for contrast, *or* is used to separate ideas that are choices or alternatives, *nor* is used to separate ideas that are negative choices, and *for* is used to show the cause or proof of a statement.

- Other linking words, called **conjunctive adverbs** that can be used to connect simple sentences to produce a compound sentence. Conjunctive adverbs frequently used are *also, accordingly, consequently, however, moreover, nevertheless, still, then, therefore,* and *thus.* When these linking words are used to connect two or more simple sentences, a semicolon (;) usually is used before the linking word, and a comma (,) is usually used after the linking word. **Examples:** Peter is running for school office; *however,* I'm not voting for him. Cindy, my best friend, is also running; *therefore,* I'm voting for her.

- If simple sentences are closely related, they may be joined by a semicolon without a linking word to form a compound sentence. **Examples:** My father suffered a heart attack; he almost died. We worked hard; it was worth it. The joining of the two simple sentences that are related with a semicolon makes the sentence a compound sentence.

- Be careful not to write a **run-on sentence.** When two simple sentences are joined with only a comma, you have written a run-on sentence. **Example:** My brother is handsome, my sister is pretty. The sentence should have been written with either a semicolon or a coordinate conjunction after the comma. It could also have been written as two separate sentences. **Examples:** My brother is handsome; my sister is pretty. My brother is handsome, and my sister is pretty.

PRACTICE A

Directions: Put a **C** in front of the following sentences that are compound sentences and an **S** in front of those that are simple sentences.

1. _____ Plants and animals are living thing.

2. _____ The phone rang, and at the same time my doorbell rang.

3. _____ The instructor and students appeared shocked by the announcement.

4. _____ The doctor gave little hope for her survival, but he said there was still a chance.

5. _____ Some things cannot be directly observed or measured.

Check answers on page 73.

PRACTICE B

Directions: Choose the words that make the sentence a **compound** sentence.

_____ 1. Girls will read (a) boy and girl books. (b) more books than boys. (c) boy books, but boys will not read girl books.

_____ 2. At school, some of my friends (a) never do their class assignments. (b) claim they don't do their assignments, but I don't believe them. (c) seem to lie about their class assignments.

_____ 3. My instructor is a good teacher (a) and he is also a good friend. (b) and also a friend. (c) a good friend, and my buddy.

_____ 4. Going to school is important (a) to my future livelihood. (b) in spite of what my friends say, but I dislike all the work I have to do. (c) has been drilled into me all my life by my parents.

_____ 5. I need help (a) to stop drinking, but I don't want to go to counseling. (b) to stop drinking. (c) to stop drinking so much beer at parties.

Check answers on page 73.

Phrases, Independent and Subordinate Clauses

OBJECTIVE This lesson should help you recognize the differences between phrases and clauses and note the various ways that clauses can be used.

- A **phrase** is a group of related words.

- A phrase, unlike a clause, does not include **both** a subject and a predicate.

- A phrase may be used as a noun, adjective, or adverb. **Examples:** *The window* of Marcie's room was broken. (Italicized words are used as a noun.) The phrase *of Marcie's room* is an adjective phrase. My friend ate *at my house* last night. (Italicized words are an adverb phrase.)

- A **clause** is a group of words that contains both a subject and predicate.

- An **independent clause** can stand alone as a sentence.

- A **subordinate clause** is part of a sentence; that is, it cannot stand alone as a sentence.

- Even though a subordinate clause has both a subject and predicate, it is not complete on its own. It usually functions as either an adjective clause, an adverb clause, or a noun clause. A subordinate clause adds meaning to or modifies the independent clause.

- An **adjective clause** behaves as an adjective in a sentence. **Example:** *The Wastelands* by T. S. Eliot is a poem *that has become a classic.* (*that has become a classic* modifies poem).

- **Note Well:** Some adjective clauses begin with pronouns that are called **relative pronouns** because they relate the adjective clause to a preceding noun or pronoun. **Examples:** Limericks, *which often are enjoyed by children,* are supposed to be amusing. Limericks *that are funny* often are enjoyed by children. (Note that a comma is used before the relative pronoun *which* but not before *that.*) Discuss your problem with a friend *whose judgment you trust.*

  - The most often used relative pronouns are *who, whom, whose, which,* and *that. Whoever, whomever,* and *whichever* are also relative pronouns when they begin an adjective clause. At times, the relative pronoun may be omitted. The clause, however, is still an adjective clause. **Example:** On my day off, I always do something *that I enjoy.* On my day off, I always do something *I enjoy.* (In the second sentence, the word *that* is omitted.)

- **Adverb clauses** are subordinate clauses that modify verbs, adjectives, or other adverbs. As adverbs, they tell **how, when, where, why, to what extent,** or **under what conditions** about the words they modify. (See Lesson 27 on adverbs.) **Examples:** Melissa spends her vacation *wherever the weather is supposed to be good.* (The adverb clause modifies the verb *spends* telling where Melissa spends her vacation.) *While Jim performed his trick,* he distracted the audience with his chatter. (The adverb clause modifies the verb *distracted.*) I will leave for Maine as early *as I can.* (The adverb clause modifies the adverb *early.* It tells how early I will leave Maine.) Kelsey's sunglasses are much darker *than her old ones.* (The adverb clause modifies the adjective *darker* and tells to what extent the sunglasses are darker.)

- A **noun clause** is a subordinate clause that functions as a noun. As a noun, it may be the subject of a sentence, the direct object, predicate nominative, or the object of a preposition. **Examples:** *What I will do later* is still uncertain. (subject of sentence) Problems that many of us encounter is *what we will discuss tomorrow.* (predicate nominative) Kelsey realized *that she had lost Ollie.* (direct object) You can do that by *whatever method you like.* (object of the preposition *by*)

- Subordinate conjunctions can change sentence meanings. Examples follow:
  - Rowena loves going for a walk *when it rains.*
  - Rowena loves going for a walk *unless it rains.*
  - Rowena loves going for a walk *even if it rains.*

PRACTICE A

Directions: Put a single line under phrases and a double line under clauses in the following sentences.

1. My brother is going to school in the fall.

2. My parents want me to study a lot at school, but I will not.

3. I feel guilty about deceiving my parents, but I soon get over that feeling.

4. No one saw the horrible assault on campus.

5. The police captured the person in a short time.

Check answers on page 73.

PRACTICE B

Directions: Follow the directions for each item.

1. Write two independent clauses. _____

   _____

   _____

2. Write three subordinate clauses. _____

   _____

   _____

3. Write four phrases. _____

   _____

   _____

Check answers on page 73.

Complex and Compound-Complex Sentences

OBJECTIVE This lesson will help you recognize and compose complex and complex-compound sentences.

- A **complex sentence** must have one independent clause and one or more dependent clauses.
- A dependent clause is also called a **subordinate clause.**
- A subordinate conjunction usually begins a subordinate clause.
- The most commonly used **subordinate conjunctions** are as follows: *after, although, as, as if, as long as, as much as, as soon as, as though, because, before, even if, even though, if, in order that, provided that, since, so that, than, though, till, unless, until, when, whenever, where, whereas,* and *while.*
- A **compound-complex sentence** consists of two or more independent clauses and one or more dependent clauses.

PRACTICE A

Directions: Add a subordinate clause to each of the following sentences to make them into complex or compound-complex sentences. State which your sentence is. The first is done for you.

1. Maria is not happy or content. _Maria is not happy, nor is she content because she just broke_
   up with her boyfriend. (compound-complex sentence)

2. Hannah is a smart woman but not too friendly. _____

   _____

3. My roommate decided to room with someone else. _____

   _____

4. My brother is going to Australia next semester. _____

   _____

5. No one in my class received a high grade on the test. _____

   _____

Check answers on page 73.

Directions: Change the following simple sentence into (a) a compound, (b) a complex, and (c) a compound-complex sentence.

1. Pete is handsome, mean, and greedy. (simple sentence—one independent clause)

   a. _____

   b. _____

   c. _____

Check answers on page 73.

LESSON 20
Verb Tense I

OBJECTIVE This lesson will expand your knowledge about verbs and help you use the present, past, and future tenses of verbs more effectively.

Review of Verbs

- Verbs are usually key words in a sentence; they clarify meaning and add spark to the sentence.
- Verbs are telling words. They express action or states of being, and they tell about anything that happens or takes place.
- Verbs can be one word or a group of words.
- Verbs must agree in number with their subjects.
- With the pronouns *he, she,* or *it,* the present regular and irregular verbs change their form. **Examples:** (regular verb): *he* plays, *she* plays, *it* plays. (irregular verb): *he* runs, *she* runs, *it* runs.

New Information About Verbs

- **Tense** refers to the change that takes place in a verb to show the time of action of the verb.
- English verbs are either regular or irregular, which has caused great problems for many individuals.
- **Regular verbs** change their form to show tense by adding the endings **-s** or **-es**, and **-ing** for their present tense and **-d** or **-ed** for their past tense.
- **Irregular verbs** also change their form by adding *-s* or *-es* and *-ing* for their present tense, but an irregular verb does *not* add **-d** or **-ed** for the past tense. Irregular verbs have no set pattern for their past tense.
- The **present tense** of verbs shows that an action is taking place in the present. **Examples:** Kelsey plays checkers. Seth rakes the leaves. She eats well.

- The present tense is also used when talking or writing about general truths or statements that are permanently true because of their timelessness. **Examples:** Dogs are canines. Cats are felines. The Earth is part of the solar system. Shakespeare is the author of *King Lear.* Humans are mammals.

- The **past tense** of verbs shows that something has already taken place—it is completed; it has ended in the past. **Examples:** (irregular verbs—*to buy; to do*): I *bought* that yesterday. I *did* that before. (regular verbs—*to play; to want*): I *played* ball yesterday. Seth *wanted* that before.

- Two most often used irregular verbs are **to be** and **to have.**
    - The past tense of *to have* is **had** in both the singular and plural. The past tense of *to be* is **was** in the singular and **were** in the plural.

- The **future tense** of verbs deals with something that has not taken place yet.

- Certain words that help express the future tense are **will, shall, is about to,** and **is going to.**

- There is no difference in the form of regular and irregular verbs in the future tense. However, if you were to use the irregular verb **is** to express the future, and it were coupled with a singular or plural noun or with different pronouns, the verb *is* would change its form.

- Pronouns coupled with *is going to* follows:

I am going to	We are going to
You are going to	You are going to
She/he/it is going to	They are going to

- Many words signal that a certain verb tense is being used. **Examples:** yesterday, today, tomorrow, in a while, in a moment, now, later, shortly

PRACTICE A

Directions: Write the correct form of the verb for the following.

1. I (be) there yesterday. _____

2. Sean and Maria (be) there tomorrow. _____

3. Michael and Hannah (be) there last week. _____

4. He (go) tomorrow. _____

5. No one (have) his coat. _____

6. We (has) to go. _____

7. Pete and I (work) last week. _____

8. It (frighten) me. _____

9. You (be) too young to work so hard. _____

10. We (climb) the mountain next week. _____

Check answers on page 73.

PRACTICE B

Directions: Write the correct form of the verb in the following sentences.

1. Shortly, we (be) going away. _____

2. My brother (mow) the lawn yesterday. _____

3. I (is) going today. _____

4. You (is) going tomorrow. _____

5. Now (be) the time. _____

6. Marisa (seem) unhappy. _____

7. I (be) happy now. _____

8. The police (capture) the criminals soon. _____

9. Sharon (believe) in being truthful. _____

10. Seth (love) Sharon. _____

Check answers on page 73.

LESSON 21
Verb Tense II

OBJECTIVE This lesson should help you use two other verb tenses more effectively.

- To be more precise in our writing and speaking, we often use other tenses besides the present, past, and future.

- When an action has started in the past and is continuing to the present, we use the verb **has** or **have** with the past participle of the verb. Examples: They *have played*. We *have jumped*. She *has worked*. It *has stopped*. **Note:** All the verbs used are regular verbs and they all end in **-ed**.

- The past participle of regular verbs is the same as the simple past tense of regular verbs.

- The tense that uses *has* or *have* with the past participle of the verb is called the **present perfect tense.**

- The past tense is one that ends the verb activity; whereas the present perfect tense continues the verb activity to the present. Examples: Hamid and Craig *went skating* yesterday. (past tense) Hamid and Craig *have gone skating* for months on Saturdays. (present perfect tense)

- The **past perfect tense** refers to an action that was completed before some other past action. Examples: We learned that the plane we were waiting for *had crashed* in an unknown area. (The plane crash had occurred before their waiting for news of it.) Francina failed the test, even though she *had studied* hard for it. (The studying had taken place before Francina took the test.)

- Note that the word **had** is used to show the past perfect tense.
- Also note that the past participle of regular verbs is similar to the past tense of regular verbs. **Examples:** had played; had helped; had jumped; had loved; had worked
- You will have to learn the past tense and past participle of irregular verbs to use them correctly in writing and speaking. (You will meet these in a later lesson.)

PRACTICE A

Directions: If the following sentences are correct, write **C** in the blank. If a sentence is incorrect, write **NC** in the blank and correct it. The first is done for you.

1. My present instructor was working at the college for twenty years. _NC   My present instructor_ has been working at the college for twenty years.

2. The delivery person has been coming at different times every day. _____

3. This year is a good one so far. _____

4. Everyone feared that the victim has been killed. _____

5. The student said that his instructor had been upset when he came to class so late. _____

Check answers on page 73.

PRACTICE B

Directions: Choose the correct verb for each of the following sentences.

1. Speaking of her early years, my grandmother said that she (was/has been/had been) an angel as a child. _____

2. Christina explained that she (knew/has known/had known) about the problem months ago. _____

3. Mary (had been/was/has been) postponing her wedding for some time. _____

4. The airline claimed that its plane (has/had) never been late. _____

5. The hospital spokesperson related to the reporters all that was known about the strange disease that (had/has) claimed so many lives. _____

Check answers on page 73.

LESSON 22
Progressive Verb Tense

OBJECTIVE This lesson will help you recognize how to use the progressive verb tense correctly.

- If an action is ongoing, that is, if it is not fixed in time, we change the verb form by adding **-ing**.

  Examples:

  I am going. (present)
  They are going.

  I was going. (past)
  They were going.

  I will be going. (future)
  They will be going.

  I have been going. (present perfect)
  They have been going.

  I had been going. (past perfect)
  They had been going.

- The **progressive verb** tense uses the helping verb **to be** plus the present participle of the verb, which is formed by adding **-ing** to the verb.

- The present participle is formed the same for both regular and irregular verbs. **Examples:** (regular verbs): love—loving; move—moving; climb—climbing; work—working. (irregular verbs): run—running; go—going; lose—losing; do—doing; be—being.

- You will meet the present participle again when discussing adjectives (see Lesson 25).

PRACTICE A

Directions: In the following sentences change the verb to its present and past progressive forms. The first is done for you.

1. John goes to town. _John is going to town. John was going to town._

2. Maria jumps rope. _____

3. Jose climbs a steep hill. _____

4. Seth audits the company's books. _____

5. Sharon plays with the children. _____

Check answers on page 73.

Directions: In the following sentences change the verb to its future progressive form. The first is done for you.

1. They went to town. _They will be going to town._ _____

2. Jack is running in the marathon. _____

3. They talked a lot about the race. _____

4. Mike works hard. _____

5. Jennifer studies hard. _____

Check answers on page 73.

LESSON 23
Linking Verbs and Verb Voice

OBJECTIVE This lesson should help you use linking verbs and verb voice more effectively.

- Verbs can take objects, that is, they can carry over an action from a subject to an object. **Examples:** Jim drinks milk. Erin eats oranges.

- Verbs that can take objects are called **transitive verbs. Examples:** work, jump, cook.

- Nouns do not change their form, whether they are the subject of a sentence or the object of the verb of a sentence. However, pronouns change their form when they receive the action. **Examples:** She loves him. (*Him* is the object of the verb *loves*.)

- Some verbs cannot take an object. They express a state that is limited to the subject of the sentence. Some of these verbs include *to be, to become, to smell, to sound, to taste, to feel, to look, to seem, to appear.* These verbs are called **linking verbs.**

- Verbs that cannot take an object are called **intransitive verbs.**

- Even though *It is I* is correct, because the verb *is* does not take an object, most people usually say *It is me*. It would not be correct, however, to say *It is him* for *It is he* or *It is her* for *It is she*.

- Adjectives, which are discussed in Lesson 25, describe linking verbs such as *be, look, seem, taste, become, sound,* and *appear*. **Examples:** Maria is happy; Seth seems annoyed; Ollie looks cute.

- In Standard English, there are two verb voices—active and passive.

- The **active voice** is more direct than the passive one. **Examples:** Mary baked a cake.

- In the **active voice**, the subject does the action. **Example:** She plays ball.

- In the **passive voice**, the subject receives the action. **Example:** Ball is played by her.

- The passive voice consists of some form of the helping verb **to be** plus the past participle of the verb. Only sentences that have verbs that can carry over an action from a subject to an object can be put in the passive voice. **Example:** The dog *bit* the student. (active voice) The student *was bitten* by the dog. (passive voice)
- None of the sentences that have verbs such as *seems, thinks, is, feels,* and so on can be put in the passive voice because they have verbs that cannot carry over an action from a subject to a receiver.
- Some verbs can and cannot take an object. **Examples:** He *flies a plane.* (active voice with an object.) Birds *fly.* (cannot take an object)

PRACTICE A

Directions: Write **A** for sentences in the active voice, **P** for those in the passive voice, and **CN** for those that cannot be put in the passive voice. Some sentences will have both **A** and **CN**.

1. Assis is a student at my school. _____
2. My instructor reads many books. _____
3. I am not happy about that. _____
4. The muggers beat a student on campus. _____
5. She was hurt by him. _____

Check answers on page 73.

PRACTICE B

Directions: Change the following sentences into the active or passive voice.

1. The mugger hurt her. _____
2. She was beaten by the mugger. _____
3. Jim studies French at school. _____
4. Class is attended by Maria. _____
5. Kelly was hurt by his words. _____

Check answers on page 73.

LESSON 24
Verb Mood

OBJECTIVE This lesson will help you use verbs still more effectively.

- The mood of a verb refers to the way writers or speakers view the action of a verb—it expresses their mood or state of mind.

- The **indicative mood** states a fact or asks a question. This includes all statement (declarative) and question (interrogative) sentences. Most verbs are in the indicative mood. Examples: I have a lot of work to do. How much time do we have to take the exam?

- The **imperative mood** expresses a command, a desire, or an urgent request. Examples: Do it now. Stop! Please help us! Go at once to the hospital! The sentences may be punctuated by an exclamation point or a period.

- The **subjunctive mood** expresses a condition contrary to fact (a condition that does not exist at the moment) or a wish. Examples: If I *were* more mature, I probably would marry Tess. I wish I *were* in the South Sea Islands.

- The subjunctive is also used in dependent clauses in sentences expressing a demand, request, or requirement. Examples: It is important that you *be* present at the reading of the will. Your grandfather requested that you *be* there.

- **Note:** In the subjunctive, **were** is used in place of **was** for the past tense, and **be** is used in place of **are** for the present tense. However, **be** is not used very often in an "if clause" expressing a condition contrary to fact. **Be** is used more often in the dependent clause of a sentence expressing a demand, request, or requirement.

- **Also note:** The subjunctive mood usually requires the use of the conditional forms **could** and **would**. Examples: If I *were* to win the lottery, I *would* buy a house.

- The subjunctive declares a state that is imagined rather than one that is or will be a fact. The verbs of statements related to the subjunctive must reflect the unfulfilled quality of the state or action. On the other hand, if the "if clause" expresses a state of action that may come to pass, the verbs are in the indicative mood. Examples: If I am elected, I shall carry out my campaign promises. If I am elected, I will remove that person from office.

PRACTICE A

Directions: Fill in the blanks of each sentence with a word that correctly completes the sentence.

1. The hijackers demanded that their requests _____ met.

2. We wish we _____ in Hawaii.

3. She wishes she _____ a famous author.

4. If he _____ the candidate, he could win the election.

5. The people demanded that the killer _____ captured.

Check answers on page 73.

PRACTICE B

Directions: Fill in the blanks of each sentence with a word that correctly completes the sentence.

1. I am sure that you _____ finish your paper on time.

2. I _____ consider your offer, if you were more trustworthy.

3. I wish my mother _____ well.

4. Seth demanded that his money _____ returned.

5. It is important that you _____ present tomorrow.

Check answers on page 73.

LESSON 25
Adjectives

OBJECTIVE This lesson will help you use descriptive words more effectively.

Read the following sentence.

The _____ instructor was giving a _____ lecture to her _____ class.

- It is possible to communicate without adjectives, that is, your sentences would make sense without them; however, adjectives add color and clarifying details to your sentences. Our language would be rather bare and uninteresting without adjectives.

- **Adjectives** describe and limit nouns. Example: (Here is a sentence without any adjectives): The cat drinks milk. (The following sentence gives you more information about the cat and the kind of milk it drinks): The small, white, shaggy cat drinks warm milk.

- The more adjectives we use, the more specific we make the noun or pronoun we are describing. For example, instead of just saying *sweater*, we could say *the funny, old, brown sweater*, which gives us a much better picture of the sweater.

- Adjectives that describe are words such as *poor, rich, pretty, handsome, clever, bright,* and *witty.*

- Adjectives limit nouns by telling how many. **Examples:** One, two, three, first, second, third. The first person to speak was very enthusiastic.

- The more adjectives we use, the more specific we make our sentence. (Read the following sentence): *The cat meows.* (Now read this sentence): *The small, white, shaggy cat meows.* The second sentence gives us more information about the cat. We know by the description of the cat that it eliminates all well-groomed big cats that are not white.

- Adjectives can limit nouns by pointing out something. **Examples: this, that, these, those; the** (definite article); **a, an** (*indefinite* articles)

- The definite article *the* is used when we are pointing out something very specific.

- The indefinite articles *a* and *an* are used when we are speaking in general about something. Note that the indefinite article *an* is used before a vowel sound.

- It is not possible to state all the words in the English language that are used as adjectives, but nouns and verbs can be made into adjectives by adding certain endings to them. **Examples:** Here are some words that are made into adjectives by adding the suffix *ful* (meaning full of): truth—truthful, beauty—beautiful, bounty—bountiful, shame—shameful, pity—pitiful, tear—tearful, tact—tactful.

Here are some words that are made into adjectives by adding the suffix -**y** (meaning full of, having, like, or somewhat): dirt—dirty, frost—frosty, ice—icy, salt—salty, stick—sticky, heath—healthy. Here are some words that add the suffix -**less**: fear—fearless, sleep—sleepless, tear—tearless, child—childless.

- If the ending -**ing** is added to a verb, the verb can function as an adjective. **Examples:** run—running, sleep—sleeping, fold—folding, knit—knitting, talk—talking

- When endings such as -**d**, -**ed**, -**n**, or -**en** are added to verbs, the words can also act as adjectives. **Examples:** broke—broken (broken toy), balance—balanced (balanced books), damage—damaged (damaged goods), fall—fallen (fallen snow)

- Sometimes nouns are used to describe or limit a noun. **Examples:** tea kettle, rose garden, peach jam, apple tree, study hall, window sill

- Sometimes pronouns are used to describe or limit other nouns. Remember we said that pronouns such as *this, that, these,* and *those* can be used to point out things. Other pronouns are *my* (my father), *her* (her dress), *his* (his shirt), and *some* (some men).

- Adjectives that are used as proper nouns, that is, in names of countries or groups of people, should always be capitalized. **Examples:** French, German, Chinese

- When the proper nouns are names of countries, they should be capitalized. **Examples:** Indian ink, Chinese tea, French cooking, German food, Japanese art

- There are times when nouns have two or more adjectives following them rather than coming before the nouns. **Examples:** The woman, *old and limping,* almost fell. My sister, *loving and kind,* is always there for me. The children, *frightened, hungry, and tired,* were happy to be home.

- When you use adjectives in a sentence, you should place the adjective close to the word that it is describing. **Examples:** *Itchy and rough,* my wool sweater irritated my skin.

- Some ridiculous sentences result if you do not place your descriptive words next to what they are modifying. We call such words **misplaced modifiers.** **Example:** The student ran after the bus *eating ice cream.* The sentence should read: The student, *eating ice cream,* ran after the bus. The first sentence is funny because it sounds as if the bus is eating the ice cream.

PRACTICE A

Directions: Change the following words into adjectives.

1. fear _____
2. home _____
3. help _____
4. rest _____
5. fright _____

6. pity _____
7. shame _____
8. tear _____
9. tact _____
10. rose _____

Check answers on page 73.

PRACTICE B

Directions: Here are some sentences with misplaced modifiers. Rewrite each sentence correctly.

1. The man ran after the dog smoking a pipe. _____

2. The child is bouncing the ball chewing gum. _____

3. The boy took off his sweater crying uncontrollably. _____

4. The man answered the phone wrapped in a towel. _____

5. Melissa bought a new car smiling broadly. _____

6. The child was put in the ambulance burning with fever. _____

7. Mary walked down the street eating an ice-cream cone. _____

8. Mr. Jones mowed his lawn wearing a bathing suit. _____

9. The girl picked up the phone screaming hysterically. _____

10. The man climbed the stairs breathing heavily. _____

Check answers on page 73.

PRACTICE C

Directions: Write a noun that can act as an adjective for the following nouns.

1. _____ bracelet

2. _____ dish

3. _____ tree

4. _____ stove

5. _____ music

Check answers on page 73.

Comparative and Superlative Degrees of Adjectives

OBJECTIVE This lesson should help you recognize differences between the comparative and superlative degrees of adjectives so that you can use them correctly.

Do you know when to use *good, better,* or *best*? What about *harder* or *hardest?* Also what about *bad* or *worst*? Some people may have this problem because they never learned about the various degrees of adjectives.

- Degree is a measure of "how much."
- There are three degrees of adjectives—positive, comparative, and superlative.
- The **positive degree** is the simplest and most commonly used form of an adjective. **Examples:** big, little, small, tall, good, bad, pretty, hot, cold, dry
- The **comparative degree** is used to show a difference of quantity, quality, or manner between two and *only two* persons, animals, ideas, places, or things. **Examples:** Maresa is taller than Mary. Joshua is shorter than Jack.
- The comparative degree of adjectives usually ends in **-er. Examples:** higher, nicer, brighter
- To show the comparative degree of an adjective that ends in **-y**, change the **y** to **i** and add **-er. Examples:** tidy—tidier, heavy—heavier, dirty—dirtier, busy—busier
- Longer adjectives, that is, adjectives that have more than two syllables, and many adjectives that end in **-ive** and **-ish** usually do not add **-er** to form the comparative. They show degree by placing the word **more** or **less** in front of the adjective. **Examples:** She is *more beautiful* than her sister. He is *more popular* than his brother. The corn crop is *less plentiful* this year than last year. Our house is *less expensive* than that one.
- Some adjectives change their spelling to show the comparative degree. **Examples:** Bad—worse; good—better; many—more; much—more; far—farther or further
- The **superlative degree** is used when making a comparison involving more than two people or things.
- The superlative degree is used to show that the quality, quantity, or manner of an adjective is at its extreme.
- To show that something is the most, **-est** is usually added to the end of most one- and two-syllable adjectives. **Examples:** biggest; brightest, greenest; highest; smallest
- Adjectives of more than two syllables and many adjectives that end in *-ish, -ive,* and *-ful* usually show the superlative degree by placing the word **most** or **least** in front of the adjective. **Examples:** least expensive; least helpful; most foolish; most playful; least productive; most selfish

- A few adjectives change their spelling to form the superlative. **Examples:** bad—worst; good—best; many—most; much—most; far—farthest or furthest
- As in comparative-degree adjectives, adjectives in the superlative degree ending in -*y* change the *y* to *i* and add the ending. **Examples:** early—earliest; pretty—prettiest; sorry—sorriest; silly—silliest; nosy—nosiest
- The comparative and superlative degrees of adjectives cannot be used with adjectives that have absolute meanings. **Examples:** circular, round, square, dead, true, false, entire, immortal, equal, perfect. It would not make sense to say that something is more round or more square or most true or most dead. You could, however, say that something is almost true or someone is nearly dead.

PRACTICE A

Directions: Write the comparative and superlative degrees of the following adjectives.

1. short _____
2. funny _____
3. bright _____
4. difficult _____
5. expensive _____
6. straight _____
7. truthful _____
8. terrible _____
9. gorgeous _____
10. humorous _____

Check answers on page 73.

PRACTICE B

Directions: Write the comparative and superlative degrees of the following adjectives.

1. good _____
2. bad _____
3. much _____
4. many _____
5. far _____

Check answers on page 74.

LESSON 27
Adverbs Including Their Comparative and Superlative Degrees

OBJECTIVE This lesson should help you use adverbs correctly.

- **Adverbs** tell something about verbs. They usually describe or limit verbs.
- Adverbs generally tell **how, when, where,** and **how much. Examples:** The boats sailed *slowly* (how). The race started *immediately.* (when) We stood *there.* (where) She taped the paper *very* carefully. (how much)
- Adverbs can describe or limit an adjective. **Example:** Kelsey and her sister Melissa are very pretty girls. (The adverb *very* describes *pretty.*)
- Adverbs can also describe or limit another adverb. **Example:** He works very hard. (The adverb *very* describes the adverb *hard.*)
- The words *very, rather, quite, too,* and *somewhat* are used to describe other adverbs. They qualify the intensity, that is, the strength or force of the adverb—they tell *how.* **Examples:** He worked *rather* hard. (how hard?) He worked *quite* hard. (how hard?) He worked *too* hard. (how hard?)
- A number of adverbs end in **-ly. Examples:** silently, calmly, brightly, quietly, loudly. You must, however, be careful because some adjectives also end in **-ly. Examples:** the friendly dog; the stately mansion.
- There are some adverbs with both **-ly** and **non -ly** endings. **Examples:** slow and slowly; high and highly; deep and deeply; loud and loudly
- Here are some adverbs that do not end in *-ly: then, soon, often, later, afterward, just, below, now, sometimes, always, never, seldom, still, today, yesterday, tomorrow, here, there, well, almost, not, so, ever, somewhat, rather, quite.*
- Note especially that **good** and **well** are often confused with one another. *Good* is an adjective. *Well* is an adverb. *Good* is used to describe a person, place or thing. *Well* describes how something is done. **Example:** *Good* people usually do *well.* However, *well* is used as an adjective when it describes someone's health. **Examples:** Sarah works *well.* She is feeling *well.* (In the first sentence, *well* is used as an adverb because it describes how something is done. In the second sentence, *well* is used as an adjective because it refers to good health.)
- Adverbs, like adjectives, have degrees of comparison, and they are formed in the same way as adjectives. Here are some examples of the positive, comparative, and superlative degrees of adverbs: *hard, harder, hardest; early, earlier, earliest; well, better, best; proudly, more proudly, most proudly.*
- Certain adverbs such as *also, indeed, however, therefore, consequently, nevertheless, moreover,* and *then* may be used as transition words to connect one sentence to another. When the adverbs are used in this way, they are usually set off by commas. The placement of the adverbs is determined by the meaning the writer wishes to convey. If the adverb is placed at the beginning of a sentence, it means the writer wishes to give special emphasis to the sentence.

PRACTICE A

Directions: Change each of the following adjectives into adverbs.

1. sure _____
2. good _____
3. noisy _____
4. rude _____
5. cheerful _____

6. angry _____
7. critical _____
8. quiet _____
9. clear _____
10. happy _____

Check answers on page 74.

PRACTICE B

Directions: Write the comparative and superlative forms for each of the following adverbs.

1. friendly _____
2. carefully _____
3. long _____
4. well _____
5. quietly _____
6. happily _____
7. beautifully _____
8. gladly _____
9. sure _____
10. much _____

Check answers on page 74.

LESSON 28
Contractions

OBJECTIVE This lesson will help you use contractions correctly.

When we write or speak, we often combine two words or shorten a compound word. Read the following: *I'll be there soon. I'll wait for him. She* **won't** *go with us.* **We'll** *try to wait.* **Don't** *tell Sarah about that.* **Who's** *going to the party later?*

- A **contraction** is a word formed by combining two words or shortening a compound word.

- When we write contractions, we often omit one or more letters, and to show that we have omitted the letters we put an apostrophe in their place. Example: he is—he's.

- Here are some of the most often used contractions: *there is—there's, who is—who's, it is—it's, she would—she'd, he would—he'd, I will—I'll, she will—she'll, he will—he'll, it will—it'll, do not—don't, who will—who'll, are not—aren't, does not—doesn't, we have—we've, could have—could've, would have—would've.*
- Do not confuse contractions with possessives. (see Lesson 29)

PRACTICE A

Directions: Here are some contractions. Write the two words that were combined to form each contraction.

1. I'll _____
2. won't _____
3. he's _____
4. don't _____
5. who's _____

6. isn't _____
7. what's _____
8. I'm _____
9. I've _____
10. there's _____

Check answers on page 74.

PRACTICE B

Directions: Combine the following two words to form a contraction.

1. there is _____
2. we will _____
3. who is _____
4. she is _____
5. let us _____

Check answers on page 74.

LESSON 29
Words Showing Ownership or Possession

OBJECTIVE This lesson will help you use possessive words correctly.

- When singular nouns or proper nouns show ownership, an **apostrophe** (') and **-s** are usually added to the nouns. **Examples:** Kelly's coat; Mr. Green's dog; dog's coat
- If a word ends in **-s**, we do *not* cut off the **-s** in the word before adding the apostrophe. **Examples:** Charles's, James's, class's

- To show ownership for plural nouns ending in **-s** or **-es**, an apostrophe is added after the **-s**. **Examples:** our parents' home (the home of our parents); the Joneses' lawn (the lawn of the Joneses); the daisies' fragrance (the fragrance of the daisies)

- To show ownership for plural nouns not ending in **-s** or **-es**, an apostrophe and *-s* are added. **Examples:** the men's room; the women's room; the children's room; the oxen's burden; the sheep's wool

- The possessive form is usually added to the last word of a hyphenated compound word. **Examples:** mother-in-law's dinner; father-in-law's barbecue; attorney-at-law's practice; attorney-general's opinion

- To show group ownership, the last proper noun is put in the possessive. **Examples:** Candice and Dick's party; Sharon and Seth's house

- To show individual ownership, each proper noun is put in the possessive. **Examples:** Peggy's and Arron's jobs; Sharon's and Seth's houses.

- Indefinite pronouns such as *any, each, all,* and *some* when combined with *body, one, other,* or *else,* add *-s* to show ownership. **Examples:** somebody's, anyone's, each other's, no one's

- The pronouns *his, her, hers, yours, my, mine, our, ours, their, theirs, its,* and *whose* do not need an apostrophe to form the possessive to show ownership because they are in the possessive form already. **Examples:** This is *his* coat. *Whose* dresses are those? What is *its* name? Is it in *its* cage?

> **SPECIAL NOTE:** Do not confuse the contraction **it's** (*it is*), **who's** (*who is* or *who has*) and *there's* (*there is*) with the possessive pronouns **its, whose,** and **theirs.**

PRACTICE A

Directions: Put the following words in their possessive forms.

1. somebody _____

2. nobody _____

3. brother-in-law _____

4. jack-o-lantern _____

5. each one _____

Check answers on page 74.

PRACTICE B

Directions: Read the following sentences carefully. If a sentence is written correctly, put a C in front of it. If it is not written correctly, correct any possessive form errors in the sentence.

_____ 1. It's feathers are blue and green.

_____ 2. Who's is it?

_____ 3. My sister-in-law's parties are usually dull.

_____ 4. No one's coat is here.

_____ 5. This is ours.

_____ 6. We went to her party.

_____ 7. The three attorneys-at-law's offices are in my building.

_____ 8. George's and Jim's room is very hot in the summer.

_____ 9. Mark said that he used another's paper.

_____10. Aidas and Juarez's pictures are lovely.

Check answers on page 74.

LESSON 30
Verbals—Participles, Gerunds, and Infinitives

OBJECTIVE This lesson will help you use participles, gerunds, and infinitives more effectively.

- Verbals, participles, gerunds, and infinitives.
- A **verbal** is a form of verb that is used as an adjective, adverb, or noun. A participle acts as an adjective; a gerund acts as a noun; and an infinitive acts as an adjective, adverb, or noun. Even though verbals are considered verbs, they are not used as verbs in sentences. **Examples:** The _scared_ student ran for cover. (_Scared,_ which is a form of the verb _scare,_ acts as an adjective in the previous sentence.) _Walking_ fast for two hours made the older man exhausted. (In this sentence _walking_ acts as a noun; it is the subject of the sentence.) The older man met other people with whom _to walk_ fast. (In this sentence _to walk_ functions as an adverb telling why the older man met other people.)
- **Verbal phrases** include the verbal and anything else that describes or modifies the verbal. **Examples:** The _scared_ student ran for cover. _Walking fast for two hours_ made the older man tired. The older man met other people with whom _to walk fast._
- A **participle** is always an adjective.
- A **gerund** is always a noun. It is a verb form ending in **-ing** and can be used the same as a noun—as the subject of a sentence, a predicate nominative, a direct object, an indirect object, or the direct object of a preposition.
- An **infinitive** is a verb form which is usually preceded by **to**. It may be used as an adjective, noun, or adverb.
- **Do not confuse** the verbal infinitive with a prepositional phrase introduced by the preposition _to_. **Prepositional phrase:** The students came _to school._ **Infinitive:** The student knows it is necessary _to study_ for a test.

PRACTICE A

Directions: Underline the verbal in the following sentences.

1. Rushing into the theater, my sister got hurt.

2. Mary said that exercising for good health is important.

3. It is important to work hard.

4. The written report will help me.

5. Seth's avocation is golfing.

Check answers on page 74.

PRACTICE B

Directions: In the following sentences write the verbal; then write whether it is used as a participle, gerund, or infinitive.

1. The walking man met many people he knew on his walk. _____

2. The man enjoys walking. _____

3. He is going to walk to town soon. _____

4. The man said he felt tired, but he refused to stop. _____

5. Some people suggested walking more slowly, but the man said it would not be a good idea to do so. _____

Check answers on page 74.

LESSON 31
Special Usage Problems

OBJECTIVE This lesson should help you to use words such as *lie* and *lay* and *leave* and *let* correctly.

This lesson deals with a number of different types of usage problems that seem to cause difficulty for many writers and speakers. Troublesome verbs, double negatives, and idioms are included.

- **Leave—let. Leave** means to cause to remain, to have remaining, or to permit to remain *undisturbed.* Examples: *Leave* your boots outside because they are covered with mud. My parents *left* me alone in the house. *Let* means to allow or to permit. Examples: Please *let* me go to the party. My parents *let* me stay alone in the house.

SPECIAL NOTE: In the sentence *My parents left me alone in the house,* the child remained alone in the house while the parents left. In the sentence *My parents let me stay alone in the house,* the child was allowed to stay alone in the house.

- **Sit—set. Set** means to put, to place, to lay, or to deposit. Examples: He *set* the table. *Set* the book on my desk. The verb *set* is considered a transitive verb, that is, a verb that can take an object. However, *set* is commonly used to refer to hens laying eggs, as in *setting hens*. It is also used in relation to the sun, as in *setting sun, the sun sets* or *sunset.* **Sit** means to rest the body in a vertical position, usually on a chair. Examples: *Sit* down. *Sit* the child down.

> **SPECIAL NOTE:** The sentence *Set the child down* has a different meaning from *Sit the child down.* In the first sentence, the child is put down, not necessarily in a sitting position. However, in the second sentence, the child is put in a sitting position.

- **Lie—lay. Lie (lay, lain) Lie** means to rest or recline. Examples: I must *lie* down because I am so tired. Last week I *lay* in bed every day until the afternoon. I could *have lain* in bed all day. **Lay (laid, laid)** means to put down or to place. Examples: *Lay* the bundles on the table. The hens *lay* eggs. He cannot remember where he *laid* his wallet.

> **SPECIAL NOTE:** People often confuse the verbs *lie* and *lay* because of the close spelling of the two verbs. Remember when you *lay* something down, you are putting something down. When you *lay* down yesterday, you were reclining. If you *laid* something down, you put something down. If you *have lain* for a while, you have been reclining for a while.

- **Can—may. Can** means being able to do something. Examples: I *can* swim. I *can* play the piano. **May** means having permission to do something. Examples: *May* I go swimming? *May* my friends stay for dinner?
- **Teach—learn. Teach** means to cause to know a subject or to cause someone to know how to do something. Examples: My teacher *taught* the children to read and write. I will *teach* you how to swim. **Learn** means to gain knowledge or understanding. Examples: I *learned* all about rocks and rock formations in my geology class. In anthropology, I *learn* about cultures different from ours.

> **SPECIAL NOTE:** Do not use *learn* in place of *teach.* You *learn* something that is taught to you by someone or you can *teach* yourself something.

- **Affect—effect. Affect** means to influence, and it is used as a verb. Examples: He seems to *affect* my brother a lot. Your words will not *affect* me. **Effect** means the result of something, and it is used as a noun. Examples: The *effect* of the medicine was powerful. He has a great *effect* on her.
- **Between—among. Between** refers to two persons or things; **among** refers to more than two persons or things. Examples: *Between* the two of us, I will not go. *Among* all of us, I will not go.

SPECIAL NOTE: When you use a pronoun with either the words *between* or *among*, you use pronouns in the objective case, such as *me, him, her, us,* and *them.* **Examples:** Between him and me; among us

- **Double negatives.** Avoid using double negatives in writing and speaking because a double negative is actually a positive and it is poor usage. **Examples:** *Don't not do that.* This sentence really means: *Do that.* You should say or write: **Don't do that.** *I don't know nothing.* This sentence really means: *I know something.* You should say or write: **I don't know anything.**

- **Unnecessary words.** Some people add unnecessary words when speaking and writing. **Examples:** *Let us go inside of the house.* The sentence should be: *Let us go inside the house.* **Of** is an unnecessary word.

- **Idioms.** There are numerous expressions that we often use with words such as *of, by, on, for, in,* and *with.* We call these expressions used with prepositions *idioms.* Here are some examples of idioms that are often used incorrectly.

  agree to. Use this idiom when talking about a proposal of some kind. Example: I *agree to* that proposal.

  agree in. Use when discussing a principle. **Example:** I *agree in* principle to that.

  agree with. You agree with a person. **Example:** I *agree with* Seth.

  agree on. Use this idiom when discussing price. **Example:** *I agree on* that price.

  angry at. You are angry at a thing or angry about something. **Examples:** I am *angry at* the situation that is slowing us down. I am *angry about* that new law.

  angry with. You are angry with a person. **Example:** I am *angry with* Erin.

  argue for. You argue for or against something. **Examples:** She is *arguing for* her rights. He is *arguing against* that proposal.

  argue with. You argue with a person. **Example:** Sarah *argued with* her mother for a long time.

  correspond with. You correspond with a person. **Example:** Rachael will *correspond with* Sarah.

  different from. This idiom is often misused. **Example:** She is *different from* her sister.

  identical with. This idiom is also often misused. **Example:** She is *identical with* her sister.

PRACTICE A

Directions: Choose the correct word that fits the blank in the following sentences.

1. _____ your things on the table. (Set/Sit)

2. _____ on the blanket. (Set/Sit)

3. _____ your things outside. (Leave/Let)

4. The sun _____ early today. (sets/sits)

5. He has _____ in bed all day today. (lain/laid)

6. I am going to _____ down now. (lay/lie)

7. _____ that down. (Lay/Lie)

8. Mother, _____ I go to the party? (may/can)

9. He _____ play tennis very well. (can/may)

10. My teacher says that I _____ things very quickly. (learn/teach)

Check answers on page 74.

PRACTICE B

Directions: Choose the word that correctly fits.

1. _____ all those people, there must be someone you like. (Between/Among)

2. _____ you and me, he's lying. (Between/Among)

3. _____ his friends, there must be someone you like. (Between/Among)

4. I am angry _____ you. (at/with)

5. She is different _____ me. (trom/to)

6. Please take your bundles _____ my car. (off of/off)

7. I waited outside _____. (of my house/my house)

8. She seems to have a dire _____ on her. (affect/effect)

9. Try not to _____ your sister in that way. (affect/effect)

10. The _____ of the news was devastating. (effect/affect)

Check answers on page 74.

Posttest
Lessons 1–31

LESSON 1: RECOGNIZING SENTENCES

Directions: Put an **S** in the blank if the words are a sentence. If the words are a sentence fragment, put an **SF** in the blank.

1. Don't go. _____
2. Out of the woods. _____
3. Help. _____
4. Who was that? _____
5. The dog attacked the student. _____

6. Not in the school. _____
7. About the course. _____
8. Is that necessary? _____
9. The professor who helped us. _____
10. No one can go. _____

LESSONS 2–3: NOUNS

Directions: Write the plural of the following nouns in the blank.

1. half _____
2. bailiff _____
3. echo _____
4. salmon _____
5. deer _____

6. box _____
7. child _____
8. sister-in-law _____
9. passer-by _____
10. baby _____

LESSONS 4–8: PRONOUNS

Directions: Choose the correct pronoun. Write it in the blank.

1. Give it to _____. (she/her)
2. About _____ are you speaking? (who/whom)
3. Are you speaking about _____? (he/him)
4. I must admit, I like _____. (her/she)
5. Adrian and _____ are going soon. (me/I)
6. That hurt _____. (her/she)
7. Erin, Jose, Maria, and _____ are happy. (me/I)
8. Tell that to _____ you want. (whoever/whomever)
9. Neither of us has _____ car. (his or her/their)
10. Everybody must do what _____ thinks is best. (he or she/they)
11. My brother, as well as his friends, has _____ a sleeping bag. (his/their)

12. The Brown family, as one, gave _____ greeting to us. (its/their)

13. Either Joshua or David will give _____ consent. (his/their)

14. Nobody is at _____ office. (their/his or her)

15. Each man and each woman must do _____ best. (his or her/their)

16. The people want _____ food now. (their/his or her)

17. Help is on _____ way. (their/its)

18. Neither Jose nor Peter will give _____ permission for you to stay. (his/our)

LESSON 9: SUBJECT OF A SENTENCE

Directions: In the following sentences, put a line under the subject and write **S** in the blank if the subject is singular and **P** if the subject is plural.

1. The poor man could hardly speak. _____

2. My cousin and I look alike. _____

3. Alicia, Javaria, and I have the same boss. _____

4. The mystery of the children's disappearance still is unsolved. _____

5. The employees voted not to strike. _____

6. Neither person wanted to go. _____

7. Measurement and evaluation are not the same. _____

8. The children's parents are frantic.

LESSONS 10–16: VERBS

Directions: Write the correct verb in the blank for each of the following.

1. She _____ (do/does) 2. He _____ (cry/cries) 3. It _____ (has/ have) 4. Aaron and Lee _____ (are/is) 5. They _____ (worry/worries) 6. Everyone _____ happy. (is are) 7. There _____ Doug and his friends. (is/are) 8. The *New York Times* _____ many interesting articles. (has/have) 9. "Trees" _____ a poem by Kilmer. (are/is); 10. Milk and cheese _____ a good source of calcium. (are/is) 11. Measles _____ a childhood disease. (is/are) 12. Economics and ethics _____ good courses. (is/are) 13. My pants _____ mending. (need/needs) 14. He _____ everybody. (love/loves) 15. Parents, with problem children, _____ help. (need/needs) 16. Alicia, not her sisters, _____ blond. (is/are) 17. Neither Jake nor Gregory _____ a car. (has/have) 18. It _____ been fun. (have/has) 19. Either the Smiths or the Browns _____ the gifts. (has/have) 20. Each chicken _____ been inspected. (has/have) 21. The Earth _____ round. (is/was) 22. The capital of the United States _____ Washington, D.C. (is/was)

LESSON 17: SIMPLE AND COMPOUND SENTENCES

Directions: Write two simple sentences. Then write three compound sentences.

1. _____
   _____
2. _____
   _____
3. _____
   _____
4. _____
   _____
5. _____
   _____

LESSON 18: PHRASES, INDEPENDENT AND SUBORDINATE CLAUSES

Directions: Write two phrases. Then write two independent and two dependent clauses.

1. _____
   _____
2. _____
   _____
3. _____
   _____
4. _____
   _____
5. _____
   _____
6. _____
   _____

LESSON 19: COMPLEX AND COMPOUND-COMPLEX SENTENCES

Directions: Write two complex sentences. Then write two compound-complex sentences.

1. _____
   _____
2. _____
   _____

3. _____

_____

4. _____

_____

LESSONS 20–22: VERB TENSES

Directions: Write the verb that correctly completes the sentence in the blank.

1. History _____ an interesting subject. (is/was)

2. _____ they still speaking to one another? (Are/Were)

3. Dogs _____ canines. (are/were)

4. Jose _____ golf next week. (plays/will play/played)

5. Spinach _____ iron. (has/had)

6. I _____ met the victim ten years ago. (has/had)

7. I _____ going to that doctor for years. (have been/had been)

8. Recently, more descriptive sex scenes in movies _____ increasing. (had been/have been)

9. It appeared from the autopsy that the victim _____ killed about three days earlier. (was/has been/ had been)

10. We heard what _____ happened. (has/had)

LESSONS 23–24: LINKING VERBS, VERB VOICE, AND VERB MOOD

Directions: Here are a number of sentences. If a sentence is correct, put a C in the blank. If it is incorrect, correct the sentence.

1. That is her. _____

2. Tell him the truth. _____

3. In the story, the frog changed into a prince. _____

4. Give him the keys. _____

5. If I was to receive the reward, I would be very happy. _____

6. The mayor demanded that I be present. _____

7. If I were a millionaire, I will help others. _____

8. I wish I was in some other place. _____

LESSON 25: ADJECTIVES

Directions: Change the following words into adjectives.

1. ice _____

2. dirt _____

3. love _____

4. show _____

5. friend_____

LESSON 26: COMPARATIVE AND SUPERLATIVE DEGREES OF ADJECTIVES

Directions: Write the comparative and superlative degrees of the following adjectives.

1. bad _____; _____

2. good _____; _____

3. bright _____; _____

4. crazy _____; _____

5. sorry _____; _____

LESSON 27: ADVERBS

Directions: Change the following adjectives into adverbs.

1. good _____

2. noisy _____

3. angry _____

4. rude _____

5. happy _____

LESSON 28: CONTRACTIONS

Directions: Write the contractions for the following.

1. there is _____

2. I am _____

3. who is _____

4. there are _____

5. does not _____

6. let us _____

7. you are _____

8. I will _____

LESSON 29: WORDS SHOWING OWNERSHIP OR POSSESSION

Directions: Write the possessive form for each of the following words.

1. woman _____

2. father-in-law _____

3. James _____

4. Ms. Lass _____

5. knife _____

LESSON 30: VERBALS

Directions: Underline the verbal(s) in the following sentences. Then state whether it is used as a participle, gerund, or infinitive.

1. The frightened child started to cry. _____

2. The running boy said he was exhausted. _____

3. Walking is good for you. _____

4. Sleeping on weekends is what I need to do. _____

5. I like to visit friendly people. _____

LESSON 31: SPECIAL USAGE PROBLEMS

Directions: Put a **C** in the blank if the sentence is correct. If not, correct the sentence.

1. I will admit it was not a good idea. _____

2. Take the trash off of the chair. _____

3. Ted don't know nothing. _____

4. He can't do anything. _____

5. I will take the brush out of the pail. _____

Check answers for posttest on page 74.

APPENDIX I
Irregular Verbs

- Regular verbs add **-s** or **-es** to form the present tense, and they add **-d** or **-ed** to form the past and the past participle. For regular verbs, the past and past participle are spelled the same. **Example:** Present tense—*jump*; Past tense—*jumped*; Past participle—*jumped*. Present tense—*she, he, it jumps*; Past tense—*they jumped*.

- Irregular verbs do not have a regular pattern for forming their past tense. Also, the past participle of an irregular verb is always used with a helping verb such as **to have**. The most often used irregular verb is probably **to be**. Consequently, the present and past tenses of the verb *to be* used with pronouns is given below. The past participle of *to be* is **been**.

- Present tense of *to be* with pronouns:

I am	we are
you are	you are
she, he, it is	they are

- Past tense of *to be* with pronouns:

I was	we were
you were	you were
she, he, it was	they were

- Some irregular verbs such as **beat** are the same in both the present tense and the past tense. The sentence, however, helps you determine the tense of the verb.

  Example:

  She *beats* him. (present tense)

  She *beat* him. (past tense)

  In the first sentence, you know it is the present tense because of the letter **-s**. In the second sentence, *She beat him*, you know that it must be in the past, even though there is no adverb such as *yesterday* because the past tense does not have the **-s**.

- However, with all other pronouns, except with *he, she,* or *it*, the verb *beat* is the same in the present tense and the past tense.

  Examples:

I beat him (present tense)	I beat him (past tense)
you beat him	you beat him
we beat him	we beat him
you beat him	you beat him
they beat him	they beat him

- **Note:** The past participle is used with the auxiliary (helping) verb **to have**. The present perfect tense is used with the present tense of *to have*, whereas the past participle is used with the past tense of *to have* to form the past perfect tense.

Examples:

He *has cut* himself. (present perfect tense)

He *had cut* himself. (past perfect tense)

Here is a list of some of the most often used irregular verbs that have similar forms in different tenses:

Present	Past	Past Participle
bet	bet	bet
catch	caught	caught
cost	cost	cost
come	came	come
cut	cut	cut
flee	fled	fled
hit	hit	hit
lay	laid	laid
lead	led	led
leave	left	left
let	let	let
lie	lied	lied
lose	lost	lost
put	put	put
set	set	set
shut	shut	shut
sit	sat	sat
slide	slid	slid
stand	stood	stood
swing	swung	swung
win	won	won

Here are some more irregular verbs. **Note:** All three tenses have different forms.

Present	Past	Past Participle
begin	began	begun
bite	bit	bitten
blow	blew	blown
break	broke	broken
choose	chose	chosen
do	did	done
drink	drank	drunk
drive	drove	driven
eat	ate	eaten
fall	fell	fallen

Present	Past	Past Participle
forget	forgot	forgotten
freeze	froze	frozen
grow	grew	grown
know	knew	known
lie (recline)	lay	lain
ride	rode	ridden
ring	rang	rung
rise	rose	risen
see	saw	seen
shake	shook	shaken
shrink	shrank	shrunk
speak	spoke	spoken
steal	stole	stolen
swim	swam	swum
take	took	taken
tear	tore	torn
throw	threw	thrown
wear	wore	worn
write	wrote	written

Brackets

Brackets ([ ]) are used to enclose a comment, explanation, definition, and so on in quoted material that is being reported or edited. **Example:** The author [Samuel Clemens] in his book *Huckleberry Finn* explores the theme of man's inhumanity to man.

Colon

A **colon** (:) is used in a formal sense to show that something is to follow. Following are examples of when a colon is used.

1. To introduce a list. **Example:** The laundry list includes these items: pillows, sheets, and towels.
2. After a formal heading. **Example:** *Dear Sir:*
3. In writing time. **Example:** 3:00 P.M.
4. To introduce a long quotation. **Example:** The judge made the following statement: "Based on all the evidence presented here, it seems in that the jurors have but one verdict that they should bring in. However . . ."
5. In a title to separate parts of the title. **Example:** "Hallucinatory Drugs: Their Effects on Drivers"

Comma

The **comma** (,) is the most often used punctuation mark. A comma signals a slight pause. This pause is not as strong as the stop signaled by a period (.) or a semicolon (;).

1. The comma helps writers shorten sentences. It replaces *and* in a series.

   Examples:
   The cake is good and the ice cream is good and the soda is good.
   The cake, ice cream, and soda are good.

   The men swam and hiked and hunted.
   The men swam, hiked, and hunted.

   The child is well mannered and smart and pretty.
   The well mannered, smart child is pretty.
2. The comma is usually used in a compound sentence to separate long independent clauses joined by conjunctions (linking words) such as *and, but, for, or, yet* and *nor.* **Example:** Sharon is a good swimmer, *but* she doesn't like to dive. Seth is a good swimmer, *and* he likes to dive.
3. A comma is *not* used in a simple sentence to separate two different predicates. **Example:** They went to a movie and then dined at a restaurant.

4. A comma is usually used after a dependent clause (an element that cannot stand alone as a sentence) when it comes before an independent clause in a complex sentence. **Example:** Although she married a wealthy man, she continued to work.

5. A comma is *not* used in a complex sentence when the independent clause comes before the dependent clause and the dependent clause is nonrestrictive. **Example:** We felt badly that you could not come with us. We didn't go because it had started to rain.

6. A comma is usually used to set off such words as *also, moreover, therefore, then, nevertheless, likewise,* and *however* unless these words are used to join independent clauses. **Examples:** *Nevertheless,* you may stay here. *However,* that is not a good idea. See also *Semicolon.*

7. A comma is *not* used after *said* if there is no direct quotation. **Examples:** (Direct quotation): She said, "Hello." (Indirect quotation): She said that she was sorry.

8. A comma is *not* used between a subject and a verb. **Example:** They need money to pay the rent.

9. A comma is *not* used before the first item in a series. **Example:** I enjoy reading, writing, and athletics.

10. When two sentences are combined with only a comma and without a linking word, the writer is making a **run-on sentence error. Example:** It stopped raining, we went outside. Possible corrections: It stopped raining; we went outside. When it stopped raining, we went outside. Since it stopped raining, we went outside. It stopped raining. We went outside.

11. A comma is *not* used between an adjective and a noun that acts as an adjective. **Examples:** big kitchen sink; pretty rose garden; large tea kettle

12. Usually a comma is not placed before descriptive words that refer to size or age. **Example:** The nice little old lady.

13. Commas are used to set off nonrestrictive modifiers (modifiers that give additional or unnecessary information in a sentence) from the rest of the sentence. **Example:** Mr. Jones, *our physical education teacher,* gives us a tremendous workout each gym period.

14. Commas are *not* used to set off restrictive modifiers (modifiers that give essential information to the thought of the sentence). **Example:** The student *who was cheating* was sent to the Dean's office.

Dash

The **dash** (–) is used to indicate some kind of break, and it is less limited than other punctuation marks. Following are some uses of the dash.

1. Used to show an abrupt shift in thought. **Example:** Yes, that is pretty—but did I tell you the news?

2. Used for suspense or emphasis. **Example:** The tapping of the cane came closer—closer.

3. Used to summarize or rephrase part of a sentence that came before. **Example:** The limping, frail old man in torn and tattered clothes, staggered down the street—a sad sight to behold.

4. Used in place of parentheses. **Example:** Fratricide—the killing of a brother or sister—is an especially horrible crime.

5. Used to show that a sentence is not finished. **Example:** I really can't say, but—

Exclamation Mark

The **exclamation mark (!)** is used at the end of an exclamatory sentence. **Example:** That is beautiful! See also *Interjection* in the Glossary.

Parentheses

Parentheses ( ) are generally used to enclose added material such as an explanation, a comment, or an elaboration of something in an already completed sentence. Some other uses are to enclose numbers, symbols, or sums that are repeated in the sentence. **Example:** The check for three hundred dollars ($300.00) should arrive tomorrow.

Period

The **period (.)** is used at the end of a declarative (statement) sentence. It is also usually used at the end of an imperative (command) sentence. **Examples:** I am a college freshman. Stop hitting him.

Question Mark

A **question mark (?)** is used at the end of an interrogative (question) sentence. **Example:** What is his name?

Quotation Marks

A direct quotation is always enclosed in **quotation marks (" ")**; there is a comma after the word *said,* and the first word of the quotation is capitalized. An indirect quotation is not enclosed in quotation marks. **Examples:** She said, "I'm enjoying myself here." She said that she is enjoying herself here.

1. Separate sentences that follow one another and are part of the same speech should be enclosed in the same pair of quotation marks. **Example:** Mary said, "Please don't go yet. Stay a little while longer."

2. Sentences that follow one another but are not part of the same speech should be enclosed in separate quotation marks. **Example:** The following questions were asked by the students: "When will we have our midterm?" "Will we have a final?" "Will you ask us to do a paper?"

3. If the words *she said* or *he said* occur in the middle of a quotation, *she said* or *he said* should not be included within the quotation marks. **Example:** "If that's true," he said, "I can't go with you."

4. If the quotation coming before *she said* or *he said* forms a complete sentence, a period should come after *she said* or *he said* **Example:** "That is a beautiful gown," she said. "I think that I'll get one just like it."

5. If the quotation comes before *he said* or *she said,* a comma usually separates the quotation from *he said* or *she said,* unless the quotation is a question or exclamation. **Examples:** "I love to travel," he said. "Oh no!" he exclaimed.

6. If the expression *he said* or *she said* comes in the middle of a question or exclamation, the exclamation mark or question mark is placed at the end of the quotation. **Example:** "That is so marvelous," she exclaimed, "that I can't wait to hear all about it!"

7. If omitted material designated by **ellipsis (. . .)** is part of the quotation, the ellipsis should be included within the quotation marks. **Example:** Alexander Pope said, "A little learning is a dangerous thing. Drink deep. . . ."

8. A quotation within a quotation is designated by single quotation marks. **Example:** The captain said, "When the shipwrecked man came aboard, he said, 'I never thought I'd see human beings again.'"

9. When you use an author's exact words in your writing, the author's words should be enclosed in quotation marks. If the quote in a sentence that comes in the middle of your sentence and it fits into what you are writing, the quote does not need a capital or a period. **Example:** I agree with Sylvia Ashton-Warner when she says that "the mind of a five-year old is as a volcano with two vents, destructiveness and creativeness," but I'm not sure how many others do.

10. Titles of poems (except long poems such as epics), stories, articles, and chapters are put in quotation marks. **Examples:** "The Monkey's Paw"; "How to Study."

11. Quotation marks are used when defining a word. **Example:** The word *animosity* means "hatred."

Semicolon

The **semicolon (;)** is a punctuation signal used to connect two independent clauses (elements that can stand alone as sentences). However, the semicolon is usually not used when two independent clauses are connected by such linking words as *and, or, but, for, nor,* or *yet.*

1. A semicolon is used if the independent clauses are closely related. If the independent clauses are not closely related, a period is usually used. **Example:** The children played monopoly for hours; it was their favorite game.

2. When linking words such as *nevertheless, however, then,* or *therefore* are used to join two independent clauses to form a compound sentence, a semicolon is usually used to separate the two clauses. **Example:** I left home late; *however,* I arrived at the concert before it started.

3. In special cases when a sentence has a long involved series that contains commas, a semicolon is used to separate the larger units of the sentence. **Example:** Wedding presents were piled high: silver, china, and porcelain on one table; electronic items on a second table; and unopened boxes occupied the last table.

Answers

Lesson 1: Recognizing Sentences
A. Underline sentences 1, 2, 4, 6, and 10. **B.** 1. That is fantastic. 2. Stay, if you wish. 3. Leave immediately! 4. The terrorist attack against the World Trade Center will not be forgotten. 5. My instructor is a pleasant individual. 6. Help! 7. Please stay with us. 8. Who is that person? 9. What does he want? 10. How can we help?

Lesson 2: Nouns
A. 1. Answers will vary. **B.** 1. imperialism. 2. beggar. 3. author. 4. conference. 5. maintenance. 6. lordship. 7. local. 8. attention. 9. civility. 10. mission.

Lesson 3: Nouns in the Singular and Plural
A. 1. passes. 2. clocks. 3. classes. 4. witches. 5. dishes. 6. axes. 7. pinches. 8. foxes. **B.** 1. wives. 2. fathers-in law. 3. deer. 4. salmon. 5. knives. 6. roofs. 7. elves. 8. sheep. 9. ladies-in-waiting.

Lesson 4: Pronouns I
A. 1. her. 2. you. 3. I. 4. she. 5. your. **B.** 1. she. 2. Her. 3. her. 4. her. 5. he. 6. He. 7. her. 8. she. 9. him. 10. Her.

Lesson 5: Pronouns II
A. (sample answers) 1. I. 2. Who. 3. What. 4. you. 5. She. **B.** 2. C. 3. C. 4. NC—He is happy. 5. NC—We are not going to the party tomorrow. 6. C. 7. NC—I am happy. 8. C. 9. C. 10. C.

Lesson 6: Pronouns III
A. 2. NC—me. 3. NC—her. 4. NC—I. 5. NC—whom. 6. C. 7. C. 8. NC—me. 9. NC—whomever. 10. C. **B.** 1. me. 2. whom. 3. I. 4. me. 5. Him.

Lesson 7: Pronouns IV
A. 1. whom. 2. We. 3. Whose. 4. yours. 5. Her. **B.** 1. C. 2. NC—Whom. 3. C. 4. NC—me. 5. C.

Lesson 8: Pronouns and Agreement, Including Sexism
A. 1. it. 2. his. 3. their. 4. his or her. 5. their; they. 6. her. 7. himself or herself; his or her. 8. their; they; her. 9. his or her; him or her. 10. its. **B.** 1. their. 2. his or her. 3. his or her. 4. their. 5. their. 6. her; she; her, 7. his or her. 8. his or her; his or her. 9. Our. 10. they; their.

Review Practice on Pronouns
1. NC—Everybody knew beforehand what he or she was supposed to say. 2. C. 3. NC—If you see anyone I know, please tell him or her "hello" for me. 4. NC—Neither John nor Carlos is going to the party. 5. C.

Lesson 9: Subject of a Sentence
A. 1. Speedy. 2. Jim; I. 3. It. 4. He. 5. We. 6. Each. 7. breakfast. 8. we. 9. Speedy. 10. Speedy; friends. **B.** 1. S. 2. P. 3. S. 4. S. 5. P. 6. S. 7. S. 8. P. 9. S. 10. P.

Lesson 10: Verbs
A. 1. bark. 2. run. 3. plays. 4. play. 5. play. 6. play. 7. runs. 8. nap. 9. Help. 10. Save **B.** 1. I run; you run; I play, you play; I work, you work.

Lesson 11: Verbs as Groups of Words
A. 1. are going. 2. is having. 3. has been jogging. 4. had jogged. 5. are studying **B.** 1. Baby cries. 2. They go. 3. He does. 4. She has. 5. We say. 6. She is. 7. I wish. 8. They wish. 9. She has. 10. He is.

Lesson 12: Agreement of Subject and Verb I
A. 1. NC—wants. 2. C. 3. C. 4. NC—are. 5. NC—seem. 6. NC—am. 7. C. 8. NC—knows. 9. C. 10. NC—are. **B.** 1. is. 2. help. 3. is. 4. work. 5. help.

Lesson 13: Agreement of Subject and Verb II
A. 1. NC—is. 2. C. 3. NC—knows. 4. NC—works. 5. C. **B.** 1. is. 2. does. 3. has. 4. cooks. 5. knows.

Lesson 14: Agreement of Subject and Verb III
A. 1. There is. 2. There are. 3. There are. 4. is. 5. is. 6. are. 7. are. 8. is. 9. is. 10. is. **B.** 1. take. 2. gives. 3. is. 4. is. 5. press. 6. cut. 7. are. 8. sends. 9. deals. 10. is.

Lesson 15: Agreement of Subject and Verb IV
A. 1. is. 2. is. 3. has. 4. are. 5. is. 6. is. 7. are. 8. is. 9. sounds. 10. is. **B.** 3. is. 4. C. 5. C. 6. C. 7. C. 8. C. 9. C. 10. C.

Lesson 16: Agreement of Subject and Verb V
A. 1. is. 2. is. 3. plays. 4. is. 5. write. 6. is. 7. has. 8. is. 9. am. 10. refuse. **B.** 2. has. 3. is. 4. have. 5. C. 6. C. 7. C. 8. gives. 9. has. 10. claim.

Review Practices for Lessons 1–16
Lesson 1:
A. 1. S. 2. S. 3. S. 4. SF. 5. SF. 6. SF. 7. SF. 8. S. 9. S. 10. S. **B.** 1. !. 2. (.). 3. (.). 4. (?). 5. (?).

Lesson 2:
1. Maria; tune. 2. John; butter. 3. fox; hunt; place. 4. boys; trick; Maria. 5. Hannah; tomatoes. 6. Seth; cheese. 7. Anna; roommate; college. 8. Jim; Erin; roses. 9. flowers. 10. Sharon; phone.

Lesson 3:
1. Joneses. 2. bunches. 3. Smiths.
4. Johnsons. 5. rashes. 6. trays.
7. volleys. 8. leaves. 9.
monarchies. 10. mothers-in-law.

Lessons 4–8:
A. 1. I. 2. she. 3. who; they. 4. It;
them. 5. It; we. **B.** (sample
answers) 1. She. 2. We. 3. me.
4. I. 5. she; you. **C.** 1. NC—
Everybody knew beforehand
what he or she was supposed to
say. 2. C. 3. C. 4. NC—Neither
John nor Carlos is going to the
party. 5. C.

Lesson 9:
1. dogs—plural. 2. nobody—
singular. 3. friend—singular.
4. passersby—plural. 5. they—
plural.

Lesson 10:
1. broke. 2. are practicing. 3. have
gone. 4. played. 5. Do have to
work.

Lesson 11:
Sample answers: 1. Are you?
2. Has it? 3. You are. 4. Am I?
5. Is it?

Lesson 12:
1. are. 2. read. 3. are. 4. go. 5. am.

Lesson 13:
1. gets. 2. has. 3. wants. 4. is.
5. is.

Lesson 14:
1. are. 2. are. 3. are. 4. is. 5. is.

Lesson 15:
1. play. 2. is. 3. is. 4. is. 5. like.

Lesson 16:
1. is. 2. is. 3. are. 4. is. 5. was.

**Lesson 17: Simple and
Compound Sentences**
A. 1. S. 2. C. 3. S. 4. C. 5. S.
B. 1. c. 2. b. 3. a. 4. b. 5. a.

**Lesson 18: Phrases,
Independent and
Subordinate Clauses**
A. 1. The whole sentence is an
independent clause; *to school* and
in the fall are phrases (*is going* is a
verb phrase). 2. *My parents want
me to study a lot at school* and *I
will not* are independent clauses;
to study is a phrase. 3. *I feel guilty
about deceiving my parents* and *I
soon get over that feeling* are
independent clauses; *about*

deceiving my parents is a phrase.
4. The whole sentence is an
independent clause; *on campus* is
a phrase. 5. The whole sentence
is an independent clause; *in a
short time* is a phrase.
B. Sentences will vary.

**Lesson 19: Complex and
Compound-complex
Sentences**
A. (sample answers) 2. Hannah is
a smart woman, *but she is not too
friendly because she has been badly
hurt by many people.* (compound-
complex sentence) 3. My
roommate decided to room with
someone else, *even though I
pleaded with her not to do so.*
(complex sentence) 4. My brother
is going to Australia next
semester *because all his friends are
going there.* (complex sentence)
5. No one in my class received a
high grade on the test *because the
test was very hard.* (complex
sentence) **B.** (sample sentences)
a. *Peter is handsome, but he is also
mean and greedy.* (compound
sentence) b. *Even though Peter is
handsome, he is also mean and
greedy.* (complex sentence)
c. *Although Peter is handsome,
he is greedy, and he is also mean.*
(compound-complex sentence)

Lesson 20: Verb Tense I
A. 1. was. 2. will be. 3. were.
4. will go. 5. has. 6. have.
7. worked. 8. frightens. 9. are.
10. will climb. **B.** 1. will be.
2. mowed. 3. am. 4. will be. 5. is.
6. seems. 7. am. 8. will capture.
9. believes. 10. loves.

Lesson 21: Verb Tense II
A. 2. C. 3. NC—This year has
been a good one so far. 4. NC—
Everyone feared that the victim
had been killed. 5. C. **B.** 1. had
been. 2. had known. 3. has been.
4. had. 5. had.

**Lesson 22: Progressive
Verb Tense**
A. 2. Maria *is jumping* rope. Maria
was jumping rope. 3. Jose *is
climbing* a steep hill. Jose *was
climbing* a steep hill. 4. Seth *is
auditing* the company's books.
Seth *was auditing* the company's
books. 5. Sharon *is playing* with

the children. Sharon *was playing*
with the children. **B.** 2. Jack *will
be running* in the marathon. 3.
They *will be talking* a lot about
the race. 4. Mike *will be working*
hard. 5. Jennifer *will be studying*
hard.

**Lesson 23: Linking Verbs and
Verb Voice**
A. 1. A; CN. 2. A. 3. A; CN. 4. A.
5. P. **B.** 1. She was hurt by the
mugger. 2. The mugger beat her.
3. French is studied by Jim at
school. 4. Maria attended class.
5. His words hurt Kelly.

Lesson 24: Verb Mood
A. 1. be. 2. were. 3. were.
4. were. 5. be. **B.** 1. will.
2. would. 3. were. 4. be. 5. be.

Lesson 25: Adjectives
A. 1. fearful; fearless.
2. homeless. 3. helpful.
4. restless. 5. frightful. 6. pitiful.
7. shameful; shameless. 8. tearful.
9. tactful; tactless. 10. rosy.
B. 1. The man smoking a pipe
ran after the dog. 2. The child
chewing gum is bouncing the
ball. 3. The boy crying
uncontrollably took off his
sweater. 4. The man wrapped in
a towel answered the phone.
5. Melissa smiling broadly
bought a new car. 6. The child
burning with fever was put in an
ambulance. 7. Mary eating an
ice-cream cone walked down the
street. 8. Mr. Jones wearing a
bathing suit mowed his lawn.
9. The girl screaming hysterically
picked up the phone. 10. The
man breathing heavily climbed
the stairs. **C.** (sample answers)
1. charm. 2. candy. 3. apple.
4. gas. 5. chamber.

**Lesson 26: Comparative and
Superlative Degrees of
Adjectives**
A. 1. shorter; shortest. 2. funnier;
funniest. 3. brighter; brightest.
4. more difficult; most difficult.
5. more expensive; most
expensive. 6. straighter;
straightest. 7. more truthful;
most truthful. 8. more terrible;
most terrible. 9. more gorgeous;
most gorgeous. 10. more
humorous. most humorous.

B. 1. better; best. 2. worse; worst.
3. more; most. 4. more; most.
5. farther; farthest.

Lesson 27: Adverbs Including Their Comparative and Superlative Degrees

A. 1. surely. 2. well. 3. noisily.
4. rudely. 5. cheerfully. 6. angrily.
7. critically. 8. quietly. 9. clearly.
10. happily. **B.** 1. more friendly;
most friendly. 2. more carefully;
most carefully. 3. longer; longest.
4. better, best. 5. more quietly;
most quietly. 6. more happily;
most happily. 7. more
beautifully; most beautifully.
8. more gladly; most gladly.
9. surer; surest. 10. more, most.

Lesson 28: Contractions

A. 1. I will. 2. will not. 3. he is.
4. do not. 5. who is; who has.
6. is not. 7. what is. 8. I am. 9. I
have. 10. there is. **B.** 1. there's.
2. we'll. 3. who's. 4. she's. 5. let's.

Lesson 29: Words Showing Ownership or Possession

A. 1. somebody's. 2. nobody's.
3. brother-in-law's. 4. jack-o-
lantern's. 5. each one's. **B.** 1. Its.
2. Whose. 3. C. 4. C. 5. C. 6. C.
7. attorneys-at-laws'. 8. George
and Jim's. 9. C. 10. Aidas's and
Juarez's.

Lesson 30: Verbals

A. 1. Rushing. 2. exercising.
3. to work. 4. written. 5. golfing.
B. 1. walking—participle.
2. walking—gerund. 3. to walk—
infinitive. 4. to stop—infinitive.
5. walking—gerund; to do—
infinitive.

Lesson 31: Special Usage Problems

A. 1. Set. 2. Sit. 3. Leave. 4. sets.
5. lain. 6. lie. 7. Lay. 8. may.
9. can. 10. learn. **B.** 1. Among.
2. Between. 3. Among. 4. with
5. from. 6. off. 7. my house.
8. effect. 9. affect. 10. effect.

Posttest Answers

Lesson 1:

1. S. 2. SF. 3. S. 4. S. 5. S. 6. SF.
7. SF. 8. S. 9. SF. 10. S.

Lessons 2–3:

1. halves. 2. bailiffs. 3. echoes.
4. salmon. 5. deer. 6. boxes.
7. children. 8. sisters-in-law.
9. passers-by. 10. babies.

Lessons 4–8:

1. her. 2. whom. 3. him. 4. her.
5. I. 6. her. 7. I. 8. whomever.
9. his or her. 10. he or she. 11. his.
12. its. 13. his. 14. his or her.
15. his or her. 16. their. 17. its.
18. his.

Lesson 9:

1. Put a line under man, S. 2. Put
a line under cousin and I, P.
3. Put a line under Alicia, Javaria,
and I, P. 4. Put a line under
mystery, S. 5. Put a line under
employees, P. 6. Put a line under
person, S. 7. Put a line under
measurement and evaluation,
P. 8. Put a line under parents, P.

Lessons 10–16:

1. does. 2. cries. 3. has. 4. are.
5. worry. 6. is. 7. are. 8. has.
9. is. 10. are. 11. is. 12. are.
13. need. 14. loves. 15. need.
16. is. 17. has. 18. has. 19. have.
20. has. 21. is. 22. is.

Lesson 17:

Sample sentences: 1. My first
name is Molly. 2. What is your
name? 3. My middle name is
Molly, and my surname is Rubin.
4. My black and white dog is my
best friend; however, he barks too
much. 5. Mary did very poorly
on the final exam; therefore, she
did not do well in the class

Lesson 18:

Samples: 1. Into the woods,
(phrase). 2. According to her
neighbors, (phrase). 3. The
students went to Australia,
(independent clause). 4. We have
a fall and spring break,
(independent clause). 5. When
she left school, (dependent
clause). 6. After they left my
house, (dependent clause).

Lesson 19:

Samples: 1. After she left my
house, she went home. (complex
sentence). 2. Marietta, who is a
hard working person, is looking

for a job. (complex senten
Jacob and Michele, who ar
friends, went into the park
they played soccer. (compo
complex sentence) 4. Greg
and Michael, who are goo
friends, go to the same col
they like to study together
they usually do well on th
exams. (compound-comple
sentence)

Lessons 20–22:

1. is. 2. Are. 3. are. 4. will
5. has. 6. had. 7. have bee
8. have been. 9. had been.
10. had.

Lessons 23–24:

1. That is she. 2. C. 3. C. 4
5. If I were to receive the r
I would be very happy. 6.
7. If I were a millionaire, I
help others. 8. I wish I wer
some other place.

Lesson 25:

1. icy. 2. dirty. 3. lovely or
4. showy. 5. friendly or fri

Lesson 26:

1. worse, worst. 2. better;
3. brighter; brightest. 4. cr
craziest. 5. sorrier; sorriest.

Lesson 27:

1. well. 2. noisily. 3. angril
4. rudely. 5. happily.

Lesson 28:

1. there's. 2. I'm 3. who's.
4. there're. 5. doesn't. 6. le
7. you're. 8. I'll.

Lesson 29:

1. woman's. 2. father-in-la
3. James's. 4. Ms. Lass's. 5.

Lesson 30:

1. frightened—participle.
2. running—participle.
3. walking—gerund.
4. sleeping—gerund.
5. to visit—infinitive.

Lesson 31:

1. C. 2. Take the trash off t
chair. 3. Ted doesn't know
anything. 4. C. 5. C.

Glossary

Adjective. A word that describes or limits nouns and pronouns is called an adjective. Descriptive words make sentences less general and more specific **Example:** The short, fat, brown, shaggy-haired dog is mine. See also *Modifier*.

1. Suffixes: Certain suffixes (endings added to words) signal that a word is an adjective. By adding certain suffixes to nouns or verbs, you can change the words into adjectives. **Examples:** virtue—virtuous; beauty—beautiful; person—personable; rain—rainy. (See also 7.)

2. Positive degree: The positive degree is the simplest and most commonly used form of adjective. It does not involve any comparisons. **Example:** The big black dog is barking. The working men went home.

3. Comparative degree: The comparative degree is used in making a comparison between two persons or things. The comparative degree shows that the adjective used to describe quantity, quality, or manner is greater in comparison to some standard. To show that something is more than something else, -er is usually added to the end of the adjective. **Examples:** He is taller than she. This problem is easier than the other one.

   Longer adjectives and many adjectives ending in *-ive, -ful,* and *-ish* show degree by placing the word *more* or *less* in front of the adjective. **Examples:** more bountiful; more protective; less sluggish

   A few adjectives change their spelling to form the comparatives.

   Examples:

Positive	Comparative
good	better
bad	worse
much	more

4. Superlative degree: The superlative degree is used when making a comparison involving more than two people or things. The superlative shows that the adjective used to describe quality, quantity, or manner is at its greatest. To show that something is the "most," -est is added to most one-syllable and two-syllable adjectives. **Examples:** She is the friendliest person I know. He is the tallest person that I've ever seen.

   Longer adjectives and many adjectives ending in *-ive, -ful* and-*ish*, usually do not add -est to show the superlative degree. They show the superlative degree by placing the word *most* or *least* in front of the adjective. **Examples:** She is the most selfish person I know. He is the most powerful executive in the company. They are the least helpful salespeople that I've ever met.

   A few adjectives change completely to form the superlative. **Examples:** bad—worst; good—best; many—most.

5. Using nouns as adjectives: Nouns can be used to describe or limit a noun. **Examples:** tea kettle; kitchen sink

6. Using pronouns as adjectives: Pronouns can be used to describe or limit adjectives. **Examples:** our new car; my beautiful baby

7. Using verbs as adjectives: If *-ing* is added to a verb, it can act as an adjective. **Examples:** the running dog; the sleeping baby. See also *Participle.*
    If *-ed, -d, -en,* or *-n* is added to some verbs, they can act as adjectives. **Examples:** the broken toy; the dreaded moment. See also *Participle.*

8. After verbs such as *be, become, smell, sound, taste, feel, look,* and *appear,* an adjective rather than an adverb is used. These verbs are called linking verbs because they connect a subject with a word that in effect renames the subject or describes the subject. **Examples:** That sounds good. He appears fine. He is nice. See also *Linking Verb.*

9. *Good* and *well* are often confused with one another. *Good* is an adjective. *Good* is used to describe a person, place, or thing. *Well* is an adverb. *Well* is used to describe how something is done. However, *well* is used as an adjective when it describes someone's health. **Examples:** That is good coffee. I do not feel well. He rides very well.

Adverb. An adverb generally tells how, when, where, and how much. **Examples:** The train moved *slowly.* (how) School starts *soon.* (when) They went *away.* (where) She runs *very* fast. (how much). See also *Modifier.*

1. Adverbs usually describe or limit verbs. **Examples:** They played *nicely.* She sews *beautifully.*

2. Adverbs can describe or limit an adjective or another adverb. **Examples:** The *carefully* constructed plan was put to a vote. (*Carefully* describes the adjective *constructed.*) He drives *too* fast. (*Too* describes the adverb *fast.*)

3. Many adverbs end in *-ly.* **Examples:** noisily, busily, quietly

4. Some adverbs do not end in *-ly.* **Examples:** always, never, later afterward, today

5. Some adverbs have both *-ly* and *non -ly* endings. **Examples:** deep—deeply; loud—loudly

6. Adverbs as adjectives have degrees of comparison. The comparisons of adverbs are formed in the same way that comparisons of adjectives are formed.

    Examples:

Positive	Comparative	Superlative
fast	faster	fastest
well	better	best
carefully	more carefully	most carefully

7. Conjunctive adverbs are used both as modifiers and linking words. They connect two independent clauses to form a compound sentence. **Examples of conjunctive adverbs:** however, nevertheless, then, therefore. See also *Linking Word.*

8. Words such as *then, however, nevertheless, therefore,* and *besides* are usually called adverbs rather than conjunctive adverbs when they do not connect two independent clauses. See also *Linking Word.*

Agreement of Subject and Verb. A verb and its subject should agree in number.

1. When a subject in a sentence is a simple subject and names only one thing or person, the verb is singular. **Example:** Jane is nice.

2. When a subject in a sentence is a compound subject or names more than one thing or person, the verb is plural. **Examples:** Jim and Susan are partners. The flowers are beautiful.

3. A singular verb is used with a singular pronoun. **Example:** She is nice.

4. A plural verb is used with a plural pronoun. **Example:** They are partners.

5. When two or more singular subjects are joined by *or* or *nor*, the verb is singular. **Examples:** Neither Paula nor Paul *is* going to the picnic tomorrow. Either you or Peter *plays* the piano at the party.

6. When two or more subjects are joined by *or* or *nor* and one subject is singular and the other is plural, the verb agrees with the subject closest to it. **Example:** Jim or his *friends are shopping* for the party.

7. The verb agrees with the subject of the sentence and not with the noun in the complete predicate of the sentence. **Examples:** *Oranges are* a good source of vitamin C. *Vitamin C is* found in all citrus fruits.

8. The words *there is* should be followed by singular noun. The words *there are* should be followed by a plural noun. **Examples:** There is a lot of noise in the room. There are too many people here.

9. A singular verb is used with such words as *neither, either, nobody, anybody, somebody, everybody, anyone, someone, one,* and *no one*. **Examples:** *Either* of you *is* welcome. *Someone is* out there.

10. The words *none* and *all* may be either singular or plural. Usually, when *none* is singular, the words *nobody, no one,* or *not one* could be used. *All* is singular when it means the whole amount of something. **Examples:** *None* of the records *were broken. Not one* of the records *is broken. All is* lost. *All are accounted* for.

11. When *each* is used with singular nouns connected by *and,* the verb is singular. **Example:** Each boy and each girl is eligible to enter the contest.

12. When a sentence has a singular subject with a plural modifier (a word or phrase that describes, limits, or restricts), the verb is singular. **Example:** The price of cherries is very high.

13. When a subject is joined to other words by *with, together, with including, as well as,* or *no less than,* the verb agrees with the subject. The verb is not influenced by the words joined to the subject. **Examples:** The captain, *together with* his men, *was able* to bring the ship to safety. The students, *as well as* their professor, *are going* to the meeting.

14. A noun that is plural in form but singular in meaning usually requires a singular verb. **Examples:** mathematics, economics, physics, ethics, measles, mumps. Mathematics is an easy course for me. Ethics deals with questions of right and wrong.

15. A noun that is plural in form and plural in meaning usually requires a plural verb. **Examples:** athletics, spectacles, scissors, pants, riches. Riches are not easy to acquire.

16. When the subject of the sentence is a group of words describing a quantity or number, and the subject is thought of as whole, the verb is usually singular. **Examples:** One thousand dollars is a fair price to pay for that. Ten from forty is thirty.

17. When the subject of the sentence is the name of a television show, a book, a poem, a newspaper, a film, a play, etc., a singular verb is used. **Examples:** *The Exorcist* was a frightening movie. The *New York Times* is read by people all over the world.

18. The word *it* requires a singular verb. **Example:** It is a nice day today.

19. When a sentence has both a negative and positive subject, the verb agrees with the subject in the positive. **Examples:** He, not you, is going. She, not I, is washing the dishes.

Antecedent. See *Pronoun.*

Appositive. See *Modifier.*

Auxiliary. An auxiliary is a helping verb. When an auxiliary accompanies a verb, it gives the tense (time) of the verb, person, number, and so on. **Examples:** am, have, will, be, may, did. I will bake the cake soon. She is going now. He has been gone a long time. See also *Predicate of a Sentence.*

Case. Case shows the relationship between a noun or pronoun and the other words in the sentence. Case is shown by a change in the form of the word or by the position of the word in a sentence. **Examples:** The cat's fur turned green from the shampoo. (*Cat's* is in the possessive case.) The cat scratched the child. (*Cat* is in the subjective case, *child* is in the objective case.) See also *Pronoun Case.*

Clause. In a sentence, a clause is a group of words that contains both a subject and a predicate. See also *Dependent Clause* and *Independent Clause.*

Conjunction. See *Linking Word.*

Conjunctive Adverb. See *Adverb; Linking Word.*

Contraction. A contraction is usually a combination of two words or a shortening of a compound word. The apostrophe is put in place of the omitted letter or letters. **Examples:** Let us go—Let's go. Who is he?—Who's he? It is Jennifer—It's Jennifer.

Do not confuse the possessives such as *whose, its,* and *theirs* with the contractions *who's, it's,* and *there's.*

Coordinate Conjunction. See *Linking Word.*

Correlative Conjunction. See *Linking Word.*

Dependent Clause. A dependent clause is a group of words that contains both a subject and a verb but cannot stand alone as a sentence because it does not express a complete thought. A dependent clause may also be referred to as a subordinate clause. **Examples:** although he is kind; when I arrive; because I need you; that he was going; since a week has passed. See also *Sentence.*

Independent Clause. An independent clause is a group of words that can stand alone as a sentence. Each clause contains a subject and a predicate and expresses a complete thought. An independent clause may also be referred to as a principal or main clause. **Examples:** The bride is wearing a beautiful white dress, but the groom is wearing jeans and a sweatshirt. (*The bride is wearing a beautiful white dress* and *the* *groom is wearing jeans and a sweatshirt* are both independent clauses. As independent clauses, they can stand alone as complete sentences. *The bride is wearing a beautiful white dress. The groom is wearing jeans and a sweatshirt.*) See also *Sentence.*

Interjection. An interjection is a word usually used with an exclamation mark to express an emotion. It is independent of the rest of the sentence. **Example:** Oh!

Intransitive Verb. An intransitive verb is a verb that cannot take an object; that is, it cannot carry over an action from a subject to an object. It is a verb expressing a state that is limited to the subject of the sentence. **Examples:** She thinks. They are happy. He swims.

Linking Verb. Verbs such as *be, become, smell, sound, taste, feel, look, seem,* and *appear* are called linking verbs because they often link a subject with a word that in effect renames the subject or describes the subject. An adjective should be used rather than an adverb after linking verbs. **Examples:** She is my teacher. She is nice. See also *Adjective.*

Linking Word

1. Coordinate (equal) conjunctions: The most often used linking words that join independent clauses are *and, but, and, or. Nor, for* and *yet* are also used as coordinate conjunctions. **Examples:** My friend likes history the best of all her subjects, but she doesn't do very well in it. Try to do your best in it, or you will have regrets later on.

   The linking words *and, but, or* are most commonly used to connect words as well as groups of words. **Examples:** I like to eat fruit, candy, and anything else that is sweet. I will take Jennifer and Sharon with me on the trip. Joe or Jerry can go.

2. Sometimes pairs of words called *correlative conjunctions* (linking words that show a one-to-one necessary relation between two sets of things) connect independent clauses. **Examples of correlative conjunctions:** either . . . or; neither . . . nor

3. Subordinate (dependent) conjunctions: The most often used linking words that introduce a dependent clause (words that cannot stand alone as a sentence) are *although, as, because, before, if, since, that, unless, until, after, as if, as though, as soon as, in order that, even if, so that.* Other words such as *where, when,* and *while* often function as subordinate conjunctions. Pronouns such as *who, which, that,* and *what* also function as subordinate conjunctions. **Examples:** Before he went away to school, he was disrespectful, wild, and insensitive. I like her because she is a kind, considerate person.

4. Conjunctive adverbs such as *however, therefore,* and *nevertheless* connect two independent clauses to form a compound sentence. See also *Verb.*

5. Linking words such as *however, therefore, nevertheless,* and *then* act as transitional words between sentences. They are usually called adverbs rather than conjunctive adverbs when used in this way.

6. Linking words help give continuity and smoothness to paragraphs. Some frequently used linking words and phrases for this purpose are *first, before, then, next, after, now, hence, so, on the other hand, also,* and *finally.*

Main Clause. See *Independent Clause.*

Modifier. A modifier is a word that describes, limits, or restricts another word or a group of words. See also *Adjective and Adverb.*

1. A word can modify a noun, a verb, an adjective, or an adverb. **Examples:** She is a *charming, friendly,* and *pretty* girl. (adjectives modifying a noun) He runs *fast.* (adverb modifying a verb) He runs *very* fast. (adverb modifying an adverb) She is *very* charming. (an adverb modifying an adjective)

2. Modifiers can consist of phrases or dependent clauses. **Examples:** A machine that doesn't work is worthless. (The dependent clause *that doesn't work* limits *machine* to a particular one.) My sister, a genius, always gets everything right. (The phrase *a genius* describes *sister.*) We went for our mother's sake. (The phrase *for our mother's sake* describes *went.* It tells why we went.)

3. If the additional information is not necessary to the thought of the sentence, it is set off by commas. This modifier is called a *nonrestrictive modifier.* If the additional information is necessary to the thought of the sentence, it is not set off by commas. This modifier is called a *restrictive modifier.*

4. Modifiers should be placed next to or near the word or words that they modify. **Examples:** Mary, eating a sandwich, told her story. (correctly placed modifier) Mary told her story eating a sandwich. (incorrectly placed modifier)

5. A modifier can be a noun or pronoun with or without its own descriptive words that follows a noun or pronoun and gives additional information that identifies the noun or pronoun. This kind of modifier is called an *appositive.* An appositive that is a nonrestrictive modifier is set off by commas. An appositive that is a restrictive modifier is not set off by commas. **Examples:** The singer Ray Charles is blind. Margaret, my girlfriend, is very moody. (The first example is a restrictive appositive because the name *Ray Charles* restricts the noun *singer* to one particular person. In the second example, the appositive *my girlfriend* is not restrictive because it is giving additional information about Margaret that is not necessary to the meaning of the sentence.)

6. A modifier can be a word such as *however, then, also,* or *nevertheless.* See also *Adverb; Linking Word.*

Nonrestrictive Modifier. See *Modifier;* 13. under *Comma* in Appendix II: *Punctuation.*

Noun. A noun is a word such as *hat, baby, money, goodness,* or *truth.* A noun names a person, an animal, a place, a thing, or an idea. See also *Case.*

1. A proper noun names a particular person, place or thing. **Examples:** Anthony, Karen, India, Grand Canyon, Empire State Building

2. A collective noun names a group, a class, or a collection and is considered as a unit or whole. **Examples:** crowd, class, jury, gang, group

Noun Plural

1. An *-s* is added to nouns such as *cat, book, plum,* and *paper.* **Examples:** cats, books, plums, papers

2. An -es is added to nouns that end in -s, -ss, -sh, -ch, or -x. Examples: buses, glasses, bushes, peaches, foxes

3. Proper nouns (names) follow the regular rules for -s and -es plurals. Examples: Bob—four Bobs; Mrs. Smith—the Smiths; Mr. Jones—the Joneses.

4. Nouns that end in -y with a vowel before the -y add -s to make the word plural. Examples: toy—toys; day—days

5. Nouns that end in -y with a consonant before the -y change the y to i and add –es. Examples: cherry—cherries; baby—babies

6. Nouns that end in -o with a consonant before the -o usually add -es or -s to make the word plural. Examples: domino—dominoes; piano—pianos; auto—autos; solo—solos; dynamo—dynamos

7. Nouns that end in -o with a vowel before the -o add -s to make the word plural. Examples: radio—radios; cameo—cameos

8. The plural of some nouns ending in -o may be formed with either -s or –es. Examples: halos or haloes; volcanoes or volcanos.

9. Nouns that end in -f or -fe usually are made plural by changing the -f or -fe to -ves. Examples: knife—knives; wife—wives. Some nouns ending in -f or -fe form the plural by adding –s. Examples: chief—chiefs; roof—roofs; safe—safes. The plural of some nouns ending in -f may be formed by either -fs or -ves. Examples: hoofs—hooves; scarves—scarfs

10. Nouns that end in -ff usually add -s to the word to form the plural. Examples: staff—staffs; sheriff—sheriffs

11. Following are exceptions to rule patterns for plurals: *foot—feet; man—men; child—children; ox—oxen; goose—geese; tooth—teeth; mouse—mice*

12. Following are some nouns that are the same in both the singular and plural: *deer—deer; salmon—salmon; sheep—sheep; fish—fish*

13. Hyphenated compound words from their plurals by adding -s or -es to the important word in the hyphenated compound word. Usually the first word is the important word in the compound. Examples: mother-in-law—mothers-in-law; attorney-at-law—attorneys-at-law

Overworked Phrase. A phrase that has been used over and over again to describe something is called an overworked phrase. Examples: pretty as a picture; hungry as a bear

You should try to avoid using overworked phrases in your writing.

Paragraph. A paragraph usually consists of a topic sentence followed by a number of related sentences. The related sentences are arranged in some order to make sense.

Linking words and phrases such as *nevertheless, for example, however, so,* and *before* help give flow and continuity to the paragraph.

Parallel Construction. See *Sentence.*

Passive. See *Verb Voice.*

Participle. The present participle and the past participle are the two forms of the participle. A participle may be used as a modifier or as a verb. When a participle is used as a verb, it is used with an auxiliary. When a participle is used as a modifier, it is used alone. See also *Adjective.*

1. *Present participle:* The present participle of regular and irregular verbs is formed by adding *-ing* to the verb. **Examples:** running; crying; coughing. The present participle is used with some form of the auxiliary *be* to produce the progressive verb forms. **Examples:** *She is going;* they are returning; we have been studying. See also *Progressive Verb Form.*

2. *Past Participle:* The past participle of regular verbs is formed by adding *-ed* or *-d* to the verb. **Examples:** climbed; described. The past participle of irregular verbs does not follow a regular pattern. **Examples:** broken; rung; torn. The past participle is used with some form of the auxiliary *be* to form the passive voice. **Examples:** was eaten; is played; is sung; should have been won. See also *Verb Voice.*

Past Participle. See *Participle.*

Phrase. A phrase is a group of related words having either no subject or no predicate; it may lack both. A phrase cannot stand alone as a sentence. **Examples:** in the yard; at the door; have been going; for you; to me

Positive Degree. See *Adjective; Adverb.*

Possessive.

1. When singular nouns or proper nouns show ownership, an apostrophe (') and *-s* are usually added to the nouns. **Examples:** James's dog is a collie. The man's letter gave the reasons for his resignation.

2. Most biblical and classical names form the singular possessive by adding the apostrophe and *-s.* **Examples:** Jupiter's lightning; Job's hardships. Exceptions: Jesus' words; Moses' words

3. To show ownership for plural nouns ending in *-s* or *–es,* an apostrophe is added after the *s.* **Examples:** our parents' property; the girls' activities; the cherries' pits; the Joneses' business

4. To show ownership for plural nouns not ending in *-s* or *–es,* an apostrophe and *-s* are added. **Examples:** the women's room; the children's playhouse; the mice's tails.

5. The possessive form is usually added to the last word of a hyphenated compound word. **Examples:** brother-in-law's house; attorney-general's decision

6. To show ownership by two or more persons as a group, the last proper noun is put in the possessive. **Examples:** Joseph and Joan's child; Maria and Mike's house

7. To show individual ownership, not group ownership, each proper noun is put in the possessive. **Examples:** Margaret's and Tony's businesses are going very well. George's and Jim's activities are very exciting.

8. Indefinite pronouns such as *any, each, all,* and *some,* when combined with *body, one, other,* or *else,* add *-s* to form the possessive to show ownership. **Examples:** anybody's, another's, someone's

9. The pronouns *his, hers, mine, ours, theirs, its,* and *whose* do not need an apostrophe to form the possessive to show ownership. **Examples:** This is mine. (This belongs to me.) *Whose is that?* (To whom does that belong?)

Predicate of a Sentence. The predicate of a sentence is a word or group of words that tells something about the subject of the sentence.

1. *Simple predicate:* A simple predicate is the verb alone. The verb is a telling word. It expresses an action, existence, or an occurrence. It can be one word such as *go, jump,* or *cook* or a group of words (verb phrase) such as *am going, have jumped,* or *will cook.*

2. *Compound predicate:* A compound predicate consists of two or more simple predicates (verbs). **Example:** The children ran and played.

3. *Complete predicate:* The complete predicate consists of the simple predicate (verb) and the words that modify (describe, limit, or restrict) the predicate. **Examples:** John's father *is a lawyer.* George *asked for help.* (*Is* and *asked* are the simple predicates. *Is a lawyer* and *asked for help* are the complete predicates.)

Preposition. A preposition shows the relation or connection between a noun or pronoun and another word in the sentence. Words such as *about, above, across, against, beyond, over,* and *under* are prepositions.

Prepositional Phrase. The prepositional phrase consists of the preposition, the noun or pronoun, and any word or words that describe the noun or pronoun. The noun or pronoun in the prepositional phrase is the object of the preposition. Prepositional phrases are used as adjectives or adverbs. **Examples:** My mother-in-law lives *near us.* (adverb) Let's go *with them.* (adverb) The child *on the rocking horse* is cute. (adjective)

Present Participle. See *Participle.*

Principal Clause. See *Independent Clause.*

Progressive Verb Form. The present participle with some form of the auxiliary *be* forms the progressive verb form. The progressive verb form is used to show that an action is continuing. It occurs in all six tenses. **Examples:** *She* is playing; we are studying; I will be playing; he has been playing. See also *Participle.*

Pronoun. A pronoun is a word used in place of a noun. **Examples:** Jennifer is a happy child. She likes to play ball with her friend. **Examples of pronouns:** I, you, he, she, we, this, that, who, what, any, anyone, herself, himself, each, one another

1. Pronouns and their antecedents: The word for which a pronoun stands is called its *antecedent.* **Example:** The book is excellent. It is excellent. (*Book* is the antecedent of *it.* The pronoun *it* refers to *book. It* is used in place of *book.*)

2. Agreement of pronouns with their antecedents: A singular antecedent requires a singular pronoun. **Example:** Anita is going away to school. She is looking forward to it.

3. Such words as *each, any, every, man, woman, person, either, neither, anybody, everybody,* and *anyone* require a singular pronoun. **Examples:** Each person does what he or she thinks is best. Everybody is practicing on his or her own.

4. A plural antecedent requires a plural pronoun. **Example:** Some parents are overprotective of their children.

5. If a pronoun has two or more antecedents connected by *and,* the pronoun referring to them is plural. **Examples:** My friend's brothers and sisters are planning a party for *their* parents. Juan and Anna are visiting *their* friends.

6. If a pronoun has two or more singular antecedents connected by *or* or *nor,* the pronoun referring to the antecedent is singular. **Examples:** Either James or Mike does *his* own work or we do not go. Neither Susan nor Cynthia has *her* own car.

7. If the antecedent of a pronoun is a collective noun, the pronoun is singular or plural depending on the meaning of the collective noun in the sentence. **Examples:** The crowd cheered *their* champion on to victory. The crowd screamed as one when *its* idol made the touchdown.

8. Indefinite pronouns such as *any, each, all* and *some* do not refer to anything definite and may not have a definite antecedent.

9. Following are some different kinds of pronouns and examples of each:

   a. Personal pronouns: These pronouns indicate the speaker (*I, you, he, she*).

   b. Demonstrative pronouns: These pronouns point out the specific person or thing that is referred to (*this, that, these*).

   c. Interrogative pronouns: These pronouns are used in asking questions (*who, which, what*).

   d. Relative pronouns: These pronouns introduce a clause modifying an antecedent (*who, which, that*).

   e. Indefinite pronouns: These pronouns refer to persons or things not easily identifiable (*any, anyone, some*).

   f. Reflexive pronouns: These pronouns are used as the object of a sentence. They point out or refer to the same person as the subject (*myself, yourself, oneself*).

   g. Intensive pronouns: These pronouns are identical to the reflexive pronouns, but they tend to emphasize the noun that they are used with (*myself, yourself, oneself*).

Pronoun Case. The personal pronouns *I, you, he, she, it, we,* and *they* and the relative pronoun *who* have different forms in the possessive case (showing ownership): *my (mine), your (yours), his, her (hers), its, our (ours), their (theirs),* and *whose.* **Examples:** That is *my* book. (*My* functions as an adjective modifying book.) That book is *mine.* (*Mine* functions as a subject complement, that is, as the renamed subject, *book.*) She found *her* keys. Juanita is a friend of *hers. Whose* car is that? It is *theirs.*

The personal pronouns *I, he, she, we,* and *they* and the relative pronoun *who* also have different objective forms (forms used when the pronouns are objects): *me, him, her, us, them,* and *whom.* **Examples:** They took *me* for a drive. (direct object of took) The guard showed Art and *her* where to park. (direct object—with *Art*—of showed) Please take *us* to *them.* (*Us* is the direct object of *take; them* is the object of a preposition.) Paul gave *him* the money. (indirect object of *gave*) To *whom* shall I send this? (object of preposition)

Restrictive Modifier. See *Modifier.*

Run-on Sentence. See 10. under *Comma* in Appendix II: Punctuation.

Sentence. A word or group of words stating, asking, commanding, supposing, or exclaiming. It contains a subject and a verb that are in agreement with one another. It begins with a capital letter and ends with a period (.), question mark (?), or exclamation mark (!). **Examples:** They are friendly people. Go. Who are you? That is pretty!

1. Types of sentences
   a. *Simple sentence:* A simple sentence consists of one single statement that can stand alone because it expresses a complete thought. A simple sentence contains only one independent clause. A simple sentence may have a simple subject and verb or a compound (two or more) subject and compound verb. **Examples:** He won the tennis match. Jennifer and Sharon play together. The children went swimming and hiking. My mother and father jog and bicycle every day.
   b. *Compound sentence:* A compound sentence contains two or more independent clauses (groups of words that can stand alone as a sentence). **Examples:** Jim studied very hard for his biology exam, but he did not do well on it. Maria likes to dance, but her boyfriend refuses to go dancing.
   c. *Complex sentence:* A complex sentence contains one independent clause (a group of words that can stand alone as a sentence) and one or more dependent clauses (groups of words that cannot stand alone as a sentence). **Examples:** She is very popular at school because she is a thoughtful, intelligent, and friendly person. Although he is not very strong, he tries to do his share.
   d. *Compound-complex sentence:* A compound-complex sentence is made up of two or more independent clauses and one or more dependent clauses. **Examples:** He went to the food store, but he did not buy anything because he forgot his shopping list. When I need help with my homework, my father tries to help me, but he usually has difficulty figuring out the problems also.
2. *Declarative sentence:* A declarative sentence is a statement. A period is used at the end of the sentence. **Examples:** My name is Ms. Smith. I am taking biology in the fall.
3. *Exclamatory sentence:* An exclamatory sentence expresses emotion or strong feeling. **Examples:** How lovely you look! What a horrible accident! See also *Interjection.*
4. *Interrogative sentence:* An interrogative sentence is a question sentence. **Examples:** What is the average life span of a horse? Are you going to Yolanda's party?
5. *Imperative sentence:* An imperative sentence expresses a command. **Examples:** Come here. Do the work now.
6. *Parallel construction:* A sentence that has parallel construction is one in which the series of elements that have been combined are equal in structure. **Example:** During our college break we ate a lot, played, and slept a lot.

Subject of a Sentence. A word or group of words about which something is said. The subject of a sentence can be a person, animal, place, thing, idea, and so on.

a. *Simple subject:* A simple subject is either a noun or a pronoun by itself. **Examples:** Miss Smith is my teacher. She is very strict. (*Miss Smith* and *she* are both simple subjects.)

b. *Compound subject:* A compound subject consists of two or more simple subjects. The simple subjects may be two or more nouns or pronouns. **Examples:** The *Smiths, Clarks,* and *Browns* are coming to my party. *Sharon, Seth,* and *I* are leaving for school tomorrow. (The italicized words in the sentences are compound subjects.)

c. *Complete subject:* The complete subject consists of the simple subject (noun or pronoun) and the words that describe, limit, or restrict the subject. **Examples:** *The small, friendly dog* wagged its tail. *The juicy, ripe apple* tasted delicious. (The simple subjects are *dog* and *apple.* The complete subjects are *the small, friendly dog* and *the juicy, ripe apple.*)

Subordinate Clause. See *Dependent Clause.*

Subordinate Conjunction. See *Linking Word.*

Suffix. A suffix is an ending added to a word. **Examples:** -less, -able, -ance, -tion

Transitive Verb. A transitive verb is a verb that can take an object, that is, it can carry over an action from a subject to an object. **Examples:** The cat drinks milk. The man held the child. She threw the ball.

Troublesome Verbs

1. *Leave—let. Leave* means *to cause to remain, to permit to remain undisturbed, to have remaining. Let* means *to allow, to permit.* **Examples:** Don't *leave* your boots in the hall. *Let* me do it by myself.

2. *Sit—set. Set* means *to put, to place, to lay, to deposit. Sit* means to rest the body in a vertical position, usually on a chair. **Examples:** *Set* your bundles down. *Sit* next to me.

3. *Lay—lie. Lie (lay, have lain)* means *to rest* or *to recline. Lay (laid, have laid)* means *to put down* or *to place.* **Examples:** Yesterday I *lay* in bed all day because I was ill. *Lay* the packages on the table.

4. *Can—may. Can* means *being able to do something. May* means *having permission to do something.* **Examples:** You *may* go swimming. I *can* swim.

5. *Teach—learn. Teach* means *to cause to know a subject* or *to cause someone to know how to do something. Learn* means *to gain knowledge or understanding.* **Examples:** He said that he would *teach* us how to make puppets from socks. I enjoy *learning* about man's past.

Verb. See *Predicate of a Sentence.*

Verb Mood. The mood of a verb shows the way that the writer or speaker views the action of the verb. It expresses the writer's or speaker's mood or state of mind. Following are the three verb moods.

1. *Indicative mood:* Mood stating a fact or asking a question. Most verbs are in this mood. **Examples:** Are you going to the beach? I am not ready yet.

2. *Imperative mode:* Mood expressing a command, a desire, or an urgent request. **Examples:** Go. Don't do that.

3. *Subjunctive mood:* Mood expressing a condition contrary to fact (a condition that does not exist at the moment) or a wish. In the subjunctive, *were* is used in place of *was* for the past tense. **Example:** If I *were* wealthy, I'd buy a new car and house. The subjunctive *be* is used in a dependent clause in a sentence expressing a demand, request, or requirement. **Example:** It is important that you *be* present at the board meeting. He requested that you *be* present at the meeting.

Verb Tense. Tense shows the *time* of the action of the verb.

1. *Present tense:* The present tense is used to show that action is taking place in the present and to show present facts. **Examples:** The students are studying for an exam. It is raining.

    Generally, the present tense of a verb is used when discussing book reviews. **Example:** Charlotte in E.B. White's *Charlotte's Web* is given virtuous human characteristics.

    Generally, The present tense of a verb is used when writing about general truths or statements that are permanently true. **Examples:** One hundred centimeters equals a meter. Geography is a study of the earth's surface.

2. *Past tense:* The past tense of a verb is used to show that something has taken place in the past and that the action is completed. **Examples:** Yesterday, I visited my uncle. I wrote my composition two days ago.

3. *Future tense:* The future tense of a verb is used to show actions that have not happened yet. The actions will take place at a future time. **Examples:** I will call you tomorrow. He will become a father very soon.

4. *Present perfect tense:* When an action that started in the past is going on or continuing at any time up to the present, the word *has* is used with the past participle of the verb. **Examples:** He has been working for five hours on that project. She has been gone for one week.

5. *Past perfect tense:* When a tale of past events is interrupted with an event happening before the past event, the word *had* is used with the past participle of the verb. **Examples:** She said that she had quit her job a week ago. Our instructor told us that he had been a prisoner for four years in a concentration camp.

    The word *had* is used with the past participle of the verb to describe an action that was completed before some other past action. **Examples:** Before I traveled in Europe, I had toured the United States. We had heard all about him before we met him.

6. In writing sentences, the verb in the independent clause should be logically consistent with the verb of the dependent clause. **Examples:** Although she receives very high grades, she claims that she never studies. I was afraid of planes because ten years ago I had been in a plane crash.

7. If the dependent clause is introduced by a verb of thinking, telling, or saying in the past tense, the verb in the dependent clause is usually in the past tense. **Examples:** He said that he was pleased with my work. He thought that I had a very important job.

8. The tense used in a story should be consistent throughout. **Example:** The man was old and poor. He had nothing but the tattered rags on his back.

Verb Voice

1. If the subject in a sentence is doing the action, the verb is in the *active voice.* **Examples:** Tony is writing a book. Sharon typed the manuscript.

2. If the subject in a sentence is receiving the action, the sentence is in the *passive voice.* **Examples:** A book is being written by Tony. The manuscript was typed by Sharon.

3. A verb in the passive voice consists of some form of the auxiliary verb *to be* plus the past participle of the main verb. **Examples:** The ball was thrown to me. The cookie was eaten by the child.

4. Only sentences that contain transitive verbs can be changed to the passive voice. **Examples:** The cat drinks milk. (active voice) Milk is drunk by the cat. (passive voice)

5. Sentences containing intransitive verbs cannot be put into the passive voice. **Examples:** He is nineteen years old. Fish swim.

6. The active voice is usually preferred. However, the passive voice is necessary when the doer of an action is unknown or the mention of a specific subject is not desired.